W9-BZB-902

THE BEST POLITICAL CARTOONS OF THE YEAR 2006 EDITION

Edited by
Daryl Cagle and
Brian Fairrington

Dedication

This book is dedicated to the many social studies teachers who use our editorial cartoons in their classrooms. We appreciate you!

The Best Political Cartoons of the Year, 2006 Edition

Daryl Cagle, Cartoonist-Editor, Cover
Brian Fairrington, Cartoonist-Editor, Inside Front Cover
Susan Cagle, Project Editor/Copywriter
Robert A. Bartley, Copy Editor
Laura Norman, Executive Editor for Que Publishing
Thanks to Cagle Cartoons staff: Stacey Fairrington/Cartoon Logistics, Cari Dawson Bartley/Administration, and Brian Davis/Support.

Special thanks to: Tribune Media Services, United Media, Creators Syndicate, Copley News Service, and the Washington Post Writers Group.

©2005 Cagle Cartoons, Inc., All Rights Reserved. The cartoons in this book are copyrighted by the respective artists or their syndicates. No images from this book may be reproduced without written permission from the artists or their syndicate representatives.

All rights reserved. No part of this book shall be reproduced, stored in a retrieval system, or transmitted by any means, electronic, mechanical, photocopying, recording, or otherwise, without written permission from the publisher. No patent liability is assumed with respect to the use of the information contained herein. Although every precaution has been taken in the preparation of this book, the publisher and author assume no responsibility for errors or omissions. Nor is any liability assumed for damages resulting from the use of the information contained herein.

International Standard Book Number: 0-7897-3471-0
Library of Congress Catalog Card Number: 2005930262
Printed in the United States of America
First Printing: December 2005

Trademarks
All terms mentioned in this book that are known to be trademarks or service marks have been appropriately capitalized. Que Publishing cannot attest to the accuracy of this information. Use of a term in this book should not be regarded as affecting the validity of any trademark or service mark.

Warning and Disclaimer
Every effort has been made to make this book as complete and as accurate as possible, but no warranty or fitness is implied. The information provided is on an "as is" basis. The authors and the publisher shall have neither liability nor responsibility to any person or entity with respect to any loss or damages arising from the information contained in this book.

Bulk Sales.
Que Publishing offers excellent discounts on this book when ordered in quantity for bulk purchases or special sales. For more information, please contact:

U.S. Corporate and Government Sales
1-800-382-3419
corpsales@pearsontechgroup.com

For sales outside the United States, please contact

International Sales
international@pearsoned.com

THE BEST POLITICAL CARTOONS OF THE YEAR 2006 EDITION

Table of Contents

About this Book, by Daryl Cagle iv
About the Editor-Cartoonists vi
Foreword by Tucker Carlson vii
About Senator Hatch viii
Foreword by Senator Orrin Hatch ix
Conservative vs. Liberal Cartoonists x

Tsunami Tragedy 2
Bush and Russia 12
Housing Prices 20
Tom Cruise 26
Charles and Camilla 32
Runaway Bride 36
Baseball and Steroids 44
Michael Jackson Verdict 56
John Bolton 66
Pope John Paul II & Pope Benedict XVI 76
Terri Schiavo 90
Space Shuttle 102
Tom DeLay 110
Minutemen 120
London Bombing 126
Pat Robertson 138
Deep Throat 148
Roberts and Miers 162
Gas Prices 172
Newsweek 184
Iraq 196
Cindy Sheehan 208
Hurricane Katrina 218
Peter Jennings 230
In Memoriam 234
Pulitzer Prize 242
Artist Index 250

About This Book

We run the huge political cartoons website at www.cagle.com. This book is the annual, paper version of our site, with collections of the best graphic commentary on all of the top news stories of the year, 2005 … well, almost the year 2005. To get our book out at the end of the year, we "put it to bed" early, so our book is more like the best cartoons from November 2004 through the end of October 2005. We start with the killer tsunami that devastated countries all around the Indian Ocean—from Indonesia to Sri Lanka—at the end of 2004. The book ends with another natural disaster, Hurricane Katrina, which laid waste to the Gulf Coast.

Between the disasters we had a busy year. The big international story was the death of Pope John Paul II and the selection of the new Pope Benedict XVI. Other noteworthy names passed from this world, from ABC News anchor Peter Jennings to Gilligan. The war in Iraq continued as homegrown Islamic terrorists set off bombs in London's subways and *Newsweek* magazine set off an Islamic furor by falsely accusing guards at Guantanamo of flushing a Quran down the toilet. With so many real things happening in the world, Congress focused on saving Terri Schiavo, a brain-damaged woman in Florida, and the media focused on a boring and annoying woman, the "runaway bride."

We often hear complaints from our readers that editorial cartoonists are too liberal. In this book I write about why the cartoonists are left-leaning and we have forewords from two well-known conservatives, Sen. Orrin Hatch, R-Utah, and TV pundit Tucker Carlson; both are political cartoon fans.

I regret that this book is sold in the humor section of the bookstore. Editorial cartoons can be funny, but more importantly, cartoons are a reflection of ourselves, our feelings and our reactions to the news of the day—a reflection that gives us a better view of who were and how we felt as history happened. This is a history book telling the story of 2005 with the clarity that can only be found in cartoons.

—Daryl Cagle

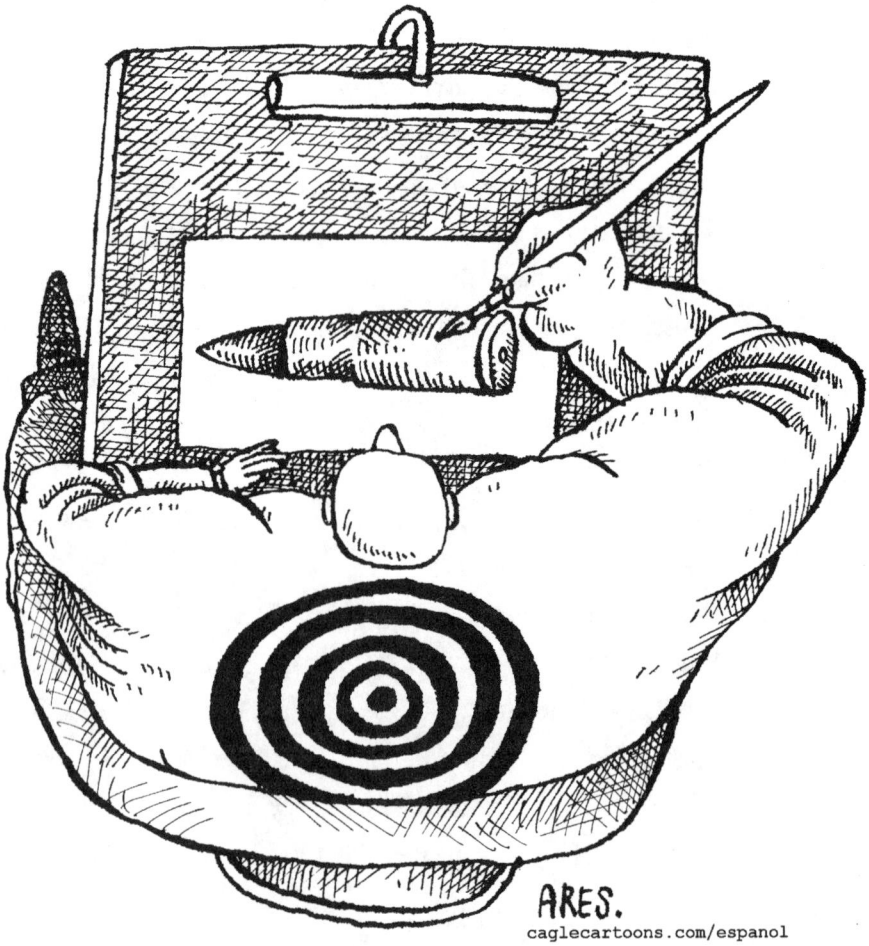

We Want to Hear from You!

As the reader of this book, you are our most important critic and commentator. We value your opinion and want to know what we're doing right, what we could do better, what areas you'd like to see us publish in, and any other words of wisdom you're willing to pass our way.

As an associate publisher for Que Publishing, I welcome your comments. You can email or write me directly to let me know what you did or didn't like about this book—as well as what we can do to make our books better.

When you write, please be sure to include this book's title and author as well as your name, email address, and phone number. I will carefully review your comments and share them with the author and editors who worked on the book.

Email: feedback@quepublishing.com
Mail: Greg Wiegand
Associate Publisher
Que Publishing
800 East 96th Street
Indianapolis, IN 46240 USA

For more information about this book or another Que Publishing title, visit our Web site at www.quepublishing.com. Type the ISBN (excluding hyphens) or the title of a book in the Search field to find the page you're looking for.

About the Editor-Cartoonists

Daryl Cagle

Daryl is the daily editorial cartoonist for MSNBC.com. With more than 3 million regular, unique users each month, Daryl's editorial cartoon site with Microsoft (www.cagle.com) is the most popular cartoon website, of any kind, on the Internet. It is also the most widely used education site in social studies classrooms around the world.

For the past 30 years, Daryl has been one of America's most prolific cartoonists. Raised in California, Daryl went to college at UC Santa Barbara, then moved to New York City where he worked for 10 years with Jim Henson's Muppets, illustrating scores of books, magazines, calendars and all manner of products.

In 2001, Daryl started a new syndicate, Cagle Cartoons, Inc. (www.caglecartoons.com), which distributes the cartoons of 46 editorial cartoonists and columnists to more than 800 newspapers in the United States, Canada, and Latin America. Daryl is a past president of the National Cartoonists Society. He has been married to his charming wife, Peg, for 22 years and has two lovely kids, Susan and Michael.

Brian Fairrington

A graduate of Arizona State University, Brian earned a bachelor's degree in political science and a master's degree in communications.

Brian is one of the most accomplished younger cartoonists in the country. Brian was the recipient of the Locher Award, the Charles M. Schulz, as well as several Society of Professional Journalists awards and Gold Circle Awards. Brian is a regular on the Phoenix-based television talk show *Horizon*, for which one of his appearances garnered an Emmy award.

Currently the editorial cartoonist with the *East Valley Tribune* in Arizona, his cartoons are also nationally syndicated to more than 800 newspapers and publications in America with Caglecartoons.com. His cartoons have appeared in *The New York Times*, *USA Today*, and *Time Magazine*, as well as on CNN, MSNBC, and FOX News. Additionally, his cartoons regularly appear on MSNBC.com's Cagle Cartoon Index.

Brian is a native of Arizona and is married to the wonderful Stacey Heywood. They have three children who act like monkeys.

Cagle portrait by John Reiner, Fairrington portrait by Brian Fairrington

Foreword by Tucker Carlson

I used to wonder when I worked at a newspaper if anyone would ever save anything I wrote. The answer, I learned, was not simply "no," but "of course not." Unless you heat your house with wood, you're not likely to keep a newspaper past the day it was printed. Except for the cartoons. People keep cartoons. They stick them to the fridge with magnets, thumbtack them to the walls of their cubicles, and send them to friends. A good editorial cartoon lives forever, or at least a lot longer than the sort of things I was writing in 1993 for the *Arkansas Democrat-Gazette*.

Cartoonists create the most enduring part of a newspaper, so you'd think they'd be heroes in the publisher's suite. They're not. A sports columnist is likely to make more money. A police reporter has better job security. For all the usual reasons (greed, stupidity, and bad taste), cartoonists don't get the respect or the compensation they deserve from their employers.

On the other hand, they are widely feared, and in the news business that qualifies as a consolation. If you've ever been the subject of a nasty cartoon, you know it hurts far more than anything that could be done to you in print. Being attacked with words is like a punch to the chest; seeing yourself mocked in a drawing feels like a jagged splinter under your thumbnail. The pain is sharp and immediate.

And yet, amazingly, people still volunteer to run for office, knowing as they do that their jutting brows, overlong chins, and funny-looking ears will be caricatured daily on America's editorial pages. Whatever else they are, politicians are an emotionally resilient group.

They have to be, as you'll see from this book. Daryl Cagle and Brian Fairrington have collected the most clever and painfully insightful drawings of the year, including some of their own work and that of other masters like Michael Ramirez and the great John Deering. Enjoy them. Clip them out and tack them to your cubicle. And remember: No matter how bad things get, at least you don't look like the cartoon version of Dick Cheney.

—Tucker Carlson

Tucker Carlson portrait by Marie Woolf

About Senator Hatch

"Peanuts" means a lot to every cartoonist. Charles M. Schulz, the creator of "Peanuts," is arguably the most successful artist of all time, with more readers and fans than any artist in history. "Sparky" passed away soon after I became president of the National Cartoonists Society (NCS) in 2000 and I oversaw the organization of a tribute to "Peanuts" in the newspaper comic strips, where almost every cartoonist drew about "Peanuts" on the same day that we gave our lifetime achievement award, posthumously, to Sparky.

Senator Dianne Feinstein of California introduced a bill to award the Congressional Gold Medal to Sparky. The Congressional Gold Medal is the highest honor Congress can bestow upon a civilian; recipients include politicians, presidents, actors and musicians, but never a cartoonist. Feinstein's office contacted me asking for help when the bill stalled in Congress. The bill was held up by Senator Jesse Helms, R-North Carolina, who felt that giving the award to a cartoonist would be frivolous. Cartoonists have never had much nice to say about Senator Helms, and Democratic Senator Feinstein didn't hold much sway with the wayward Republican. The Gold Medal bill was dead unless cartoonists could do something.

Cartoonist Marie Woolf knew Senator Orrin Hatch, R-Utah, and asked for his help in breaking the logjam. Senator Hatch is a big cartoon fan, and he jumped in and came to the rescue, twisting Senator Helms's arm and breaking the legislative logjam. Senator Hatch deserves our thanks for selflessly bringing a dead bill back to life and for bringing credit to our art form on a par with the honors that Congress has long bestowed on jazz musicians, singers, scientists, and actors.

On April 5, 2000, HR 3642, authored by Rep. Mike Thompson, D-California, who represented Schulz in his congressional district, was approved by a 410-1 vote. Thompson introduced the bill with 305 cosponsors, but we know that it never could have happened without Senator Hatch.

—Daryl Cagle, Cartoonist for MSNBC.com

Senator Hatch portrait by Marie Woolf, with apologies to Charles M. Schulz, Schroeder and Lucy.

Foreword by Senator Orrin Hatch

In 1997 I was invited to give a speech to the annual convention of the Association of American Editorial Cartoonists in Orlando. I was a little hesitant because I could wallpaper all the walls in my office with the political cartoons that have been drawn about me, and I didn't want to give a room full of cartoonists too much more ammunition.

However, through a mutual exchange of information and respect, that speech launched a wonderful friendship and professional association with many cartoonists and their industry. It might seem like a crazy comparison, but I believe members of Congress and editorial cartoonists actually have quite a bit in common. We tend to warily endure one another, uniquely appreciating our respective motivations and demands in the face of partisan attacks, responsibilities to the public, and the opportunity to influence opinion. Like Charlie Brown with the football, we keep trying, knowing that hope can triumph over experience.

I've always been a great fan of editorial cartooning as one of the great, underappreciated art forms. And knowing as we all do that humor provides an opportunity to get a little attention, I enjoyed launching a few volleys back at America's top editorial cartoonists in Orlando. We agreed that we're in the same business: power through persuasion. We also agreed that the secret to surviving our chosen professions is being able to pull the arrows out, dust ourselves off, and keep smiling.

As a professional moving target I have learned to never underestimate the importance of a good laugh. With events swirling around us of national, personal, and historical significance—humor can often diffuse very difficult circumstances. Editorial cartoons provide all of us with a snapshot of our world on a daily basis. The humor found within the drawings on the page helps us laugh for a few moments, and think for a long while.

Daryl's *Best Political Cartoons of the Year* anthology again wonderfully proves that where politics is concerned, we're all witnesses to—and participants in—the inexplicable. While I might not always agree with the characterizations presented, I am hopeful these cartoons will provide a lot of laughs and will cause readers to stop and reflect on the events that have shaped all of our lives this year. America's cartoonists remind us that in our America of the individual opinion, laughter, and perspective do flourish.

—Senator Orrin Hatch (R-Utah)

Liberal vs. Conservative Humor by Daryl Cagle

Liberals see conservatives as preachy, sanctimonious, and humorless. Conservatives see nothing funny about shrill, angry, liberal losers. Who is funny? It depends on your point of view, but humor writers and cartoonists will always be liberal-leaning; it is a bias that is built into the system. It boils down to core values.

Conservatives believe that people should be trusted; they believe that we should all take responsibility for ourselves, that we should enjoy the rewards of our personal successes and suffer the consequences of our personal failures. Liberals believe that people are basically stupid; that we should be protected from hurting ourselves by making the poor decisions that we would certainly make if we were free to exercise our stupidity. As a cartoonist, I know that I can't make a living drawing cartoons about people who take responsibility for themselves, but I can make a career out of drawing stupid people.

Elephsnt by Fairrington

The responsible-versus-stupid-perspective is clear for all to see in the Social Security debate. President Bush wants personal retirement accounts where we can make decisions for ourselves about where our money goes. Liberals don't want us to have the freedom to make the poor investment decisions that could erode our retirement "savings." There is no middle ground between responsible and stupid. The same is true with humor.

Jay Leno is a liberal humorist. Jay walks down the street and gives everyday folks the opportunity to demonstrate how stupid they are, while Jay laughs at them. David Letterman is a conservative humorist. Dave treats everyday folks with respect, giving them the opportunity to laugh at how silly Dave is, as he has fruit dropped from a rooftop, or when he visits his stoic neighbor Rupert Jee at Hello Deli with another goofy contest. Both Leno and Letterman are funny. Liberals and conservatives can both be funny, but it is easier to be funny by laughing at others, rather than laughing with others. Most humorists take the easy road.

In politics it is easy to poke fun at the people in power. Political cartooning is a negative art form. Cartoonists tear things down. There is nothing funny about a cartoon that defends the people in power. With the White House and Congress controlled by conservatives it is no surprise that conservatives are humorless.

Demographics also favor liberal laughs as the blue-state media centers in California and New York broadcast their perspectives into the humorless red states.

Editors often complain that liberal newspaper political cartoonists outnumber conservatives by a ratio of about 10-to-1. Since cartoonists are evenly distributed at newspapers across the country, why would this be true? Most editorial cartoonists rely on a full-time newspaper job because it is tough to make a living only through syndication or freelancing. There are fewer and fewer newspaper jobs for cartoonists as papers cut back on their editorial staffs and cartoonists are seen as expendable. The few jobs (about 85) that remain are at the biggest newspapers, which are usually in the biggest cities, which tend to be more liberal areas. There are about 1,500 daily newspapers in America, and the vast majority are small suburban or rural papers that are conservative and are either too small or too cheap to hire their own local cartoonist. Unless those conservative newspapers get off the dime and decide to hire local cartoonists, we're always going to see a majority of urban, liberal cartoonists.

Conservatives should learn to laugh at themselves, like David Letterman; instead they choose to complain about liberal control of the media. Rather than complaining, what conservatives need are better jokes, a more liberal attitude about their checkbooks, and most of all, a liberal in the White House.

—Daryl Cagle
Cartoonist for MSNBC.com

Donkey by Cagle

Tsunami Tragedy

On December 26, 2004, an Indian Ocean earthquake caused a series of massive tsunamis that devastated countries from Indonesia to Sri Lanka to Somalia and killed more than 310,000 people. The disaster prompted a worldwide effort to raise hundreds of millions of dollars for relief. Cartoonists reflected on the tragedy and aggravating factors, such as the lack of a warning system and the poverty in many nations that were hit hardest by the tsunami.

THOMAS BOLDT
Calgary Sun

MATT DAVIES
Journal News (NY)

MATT DAVIES
Journal News (NY)

STEVE NEASE, Oakville Beaver

CHRIS BRITT, State Journal-Register

JIMMY MARGULIES, The Record

PAUL COMBS, Tampa Tribune

LARRY WRIGHT, Detroit News

BOB GORRELL
Creators Syndicate

TSUNAMI

STEVE SACK, Minneapolis Star-Tribune

BRUCE BEATTIE, Daytona News-Journal

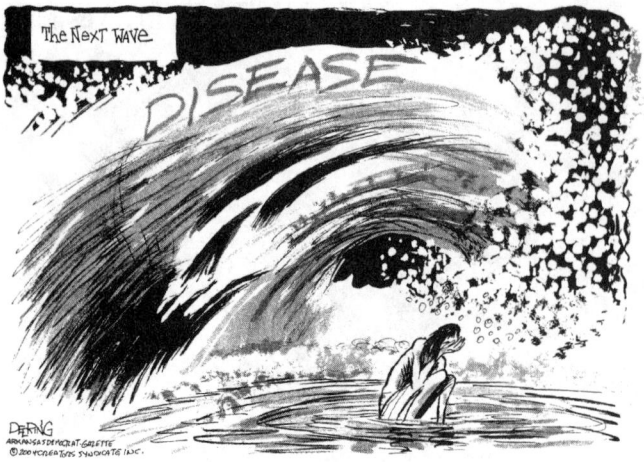

JOHN DEERING, Arkansas Democrat Gazette

CHIP BOK, Akron Beacon-Journal

DREW SHENEMAN, Newark Star-Ledger

MIKE KEEFE, Denver Post

JOHN TREVER
Albuquerque Journal

CAMERON CARDOW
Ottawa Citizen

MIKE LESTER, Rome News-Tribune (GA)

MARSHALL RAMSEY
Clarion Ledger

ED STEIN
Rocky Mountain News

JACK OHMAN
Portland Oregonian

THE ARROGANCE OF MANKIND, CHAPTER 456,773...

VINCE O'FARRELL
Australia

STEVE GREENBERG
Ventura Star (CA)

SHANNON WHEELER, Too Much Coffee Man

VINCE O'FARRELL
Australia

MIKE THOMPSON
Detroit Free-Press

OLLE JOHANSSON
Sweden

MATT DAVIES, Journal News (NY)

JEFF KOTERBA, Omaha World Herald

MIKE LANE, Cagle Cartoons

BOB GORRELL
Creators Syndicate

Bush and Russia

President Bush invited Russian President Vladimir Putin to his Crawford, Texas, ranch. Bush said he "looked into [Putin's] eyes and saw his soul." But many politicians and cartoonists saw Putin as an autocrat in the mold of old Soviet dictators and challenged the clarity of Bush's eyesight.

M. e. Cohen
(left)

KIRK ANDERSON
(next page)

THE BUSHEVIKS' GREAT LEAP FORWARD

www.kirktoons.com
KIRK 05

MATT DAVIES, Journal News (NY)

THE DRIVING LESSON

ED STEIN, Rocky Mountain News

MIKE KEEFE, Denver Post

MICHAEL RAMIREZ, Los Angeles Times

MARSHALL RAMSEY, Clarion Ledger (MI)

PUTIN and BUSH GO FOR A FRIENDLY DRIVE

SCOTT STANTIS, Birmingham News

BOB ENGLEHART, Hartford Courant

CHRISTO KOMARNITSKI, Bulgaria

DWANE POWELL, Raliegh News & Observer

JOHN TREVER, Albuquerque Journal

ROBERT ARIAIL, The State (SC)

J.D. CROWE, Mobile Register

MIKE THOMPSON, Detroit Free-Press

PATRICK CHAPPATTE
International Herald Tribune

MARLETTE © 2005
TALLAHASSEE DEMOCRAT
dougmarlette.com

ARE YOU SURE THAT'S THE TEXAS TWO-STEP?

PUTIN

DOUG MARLETTE
Tallahassee Democrat

J.D. CROWE
Mobile Register

MIKE KEEFE, Denver Post

SANDY HUFFAKER, Cagle Cartoons

ERIC ALLIE, Pioneer Press (IL)

RIBER HANSSON, Sweden

MONTE WOLVERTON, Cagle Cartoons

ANTONIO NERIL LICON, Mexico

BUSH AND RUSSIA

Housing Prices

Throughout the year, housing prices nationwide went through the roof and consumers' jaws went through the floor. Federal Reserve Board Chairman Alan Greenspan warned that the bubble would burst soon, but it only seemed to grow bigger and bigger.

ANDY SINGER, No Exit

BRIAN FAIRRINGTON
Cagle Cartoons

DAVID HORSEY
Seattle Post Intelligencer

"Overpaying for a house is OK as long as you don't use any nails doing home-improvement projects."

BRUCE BEATTIE, Daytona News-Journal

DICK WRIGHT, Copley News Service

MATT DAVIES, Journal News (NY)

DREW SHENEMAN, Newark Star-Ledger

STEVE SACK, Minneapolis Star-Tribune

JOHN DEERING, Arkansas Democrat Gazette

HOUSING PRICES

MILT PRIGGEE

NATE BEELER, Washington Examiner

JEFF STAHLER
Columbus Dispatch

SANDY HUFFAKER, Cagle Cartoons

JOE HELLER, Green Bay Press-Gazette

GARY BROOKINS, Richmond Times-Dispatch

JOHN DEERING, Arkansas Democrat Gazette

PATRICK O'CONNOR, Los Angeles Daily News

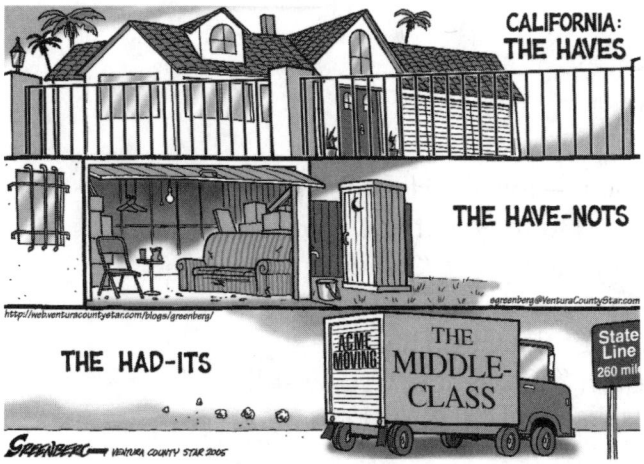

STEVE GREENBERG, Ventura County Star

GARY MARKSTEIN, Copley News Service

PATRICK O'CONNOR, Los Angeles Daily News

BOB GORRELL, Creators Syndicate

ANDY SINGER, No Exit

NATE BEELER, Washington Examiner

Tom Cruise

Tom Cruise reminded the world how crazy he is—loudly. He stood on a couch to express his love for new fiancée Katie Holmes on the *Oprah Winfrey Show*, argued with Matt Lauer that psychiatry is a "pseudo-science," and promoted Scientology with a new passion. Cruise had reportedly risen to one of the highest echelons of the Church of Scientology, the "Operating Thetan Level Seven." Somehow Cruise still manages to capture the hearts and minds of crazy, middle-aged women—and the ink of editorial cartoonists.

BRIAN FAIRRINGTON, Cagle Cartoons

DOUG MARLETTE
Tallahassee Democrat

STEVE BREEN
San Diego
Union-Tribune

SANDY HUFFAKER
Cagle Cartoons

I'LL PAY EXTRA IF THE ALIENS TAKE TOM CRUISE WITH THEM

RANDY BISH, Pittsburgh Tribune-Review

JOHN SPENCER, Philadelphia Business Journal

MIKE GRASTON
Windsor Star

JIMMY MARGULIES, The Record (NJ)

CLAY JONES, Freelance-Star

NIK SCOTT, Australia

CHRIS BRITT, The State Journal-Register

MIKE KEEFE, Denver Post

SIGNE WILKINSON, Philadelphia Daily News

PATRICK O'CONNOR, Los Angeles Daily News

"I LIKED THE PART WHERE HE TOLD THE ALIENS THAT TAKING OVER THE EARTH WAS JUST MASKING THEIR REAL PROBLEMS AND ALL THEY NEEDED WAS A GOOD WORKOUT."

DREW SHENEMAN, Newark Star-Ledger

LARRY WRIGHT
Detroit News

TOM CRUISE

JOHN DEERING
Arkansas Democrat Gazette

MIKE THOMPSON, Detroit Free-Press

Charles and Camilla

Prince Charles finally wed his longtime and much-despised strumpet, Camilla Parker Bowles, in a civil ceremony. Camilla became the highest-ranked female member of the royal family after Queen Elizabeth II, who did not attend the ceremony. Cartoonists reminded everyone of Charles and Camilla's affair as the happy couple recited vows acknowledging past "sins and wickedness."

OSMANI SIMANCA
Brazil

VINCE O'FARRELL, Australia

PATRICK CHAPPATTE, International Herald Tribune

CHRISTO KOMARNITSKI
Bulgaria

CAMERON CARDOW
Ottawa Citizen

THE POSSIBILITY OF HAVING CAMILLA PARKER BOWLES SUCCEED QUEEN ELIZABETH SETS OFF A CONSTITUTIONAL CRISIS IN BRITAIN... THE REST, AS THEY SAY, IS HISTORY.

SANDY HUFFAKER
Cagle Cartoons

VINCE O'FARRELL, Australia

JOHN COLE

STEPHANE PERAY, Thailand

MIKE LESTER, Rome News-Tribune (GA)

CHARLES AND CAMILLA

CAMERON CARDOW, Ottawa Citizen

Runaway Bride

Three days after she ran away from Duluth, GA, Jennifer Willbanks called her husband-to-be and told him that she'd been kidnapped and sexually assaulted—when she had in fact run away. The media were all over the "runaway bride," from her disappearance until well after she earned two years' probation and 120 hours of community service for giving false information to police. Cartoonists poked fun at the media circus and runaway Willbanks, as her deer-in-the-headlights expression was just too silly to be ignored.

STEVE KELLEY, New Orleans Times Picayune

WHY DIDN'T I THINK OF THAT?

George

Laura

RUNAWAY BRIDE

Englehart 5-3-05 HARTFORD COURANT.

BOB ENGLEHART, Hartford Courant

MIKE RAMIREZ
Los Angeles Times

SOCIAL SECURITY

RUNAWAY BRIDE

JOHN DARKOW, Columbia Daily Tribune (MO)

JOE HELLER, Green Bay Press-Gazette

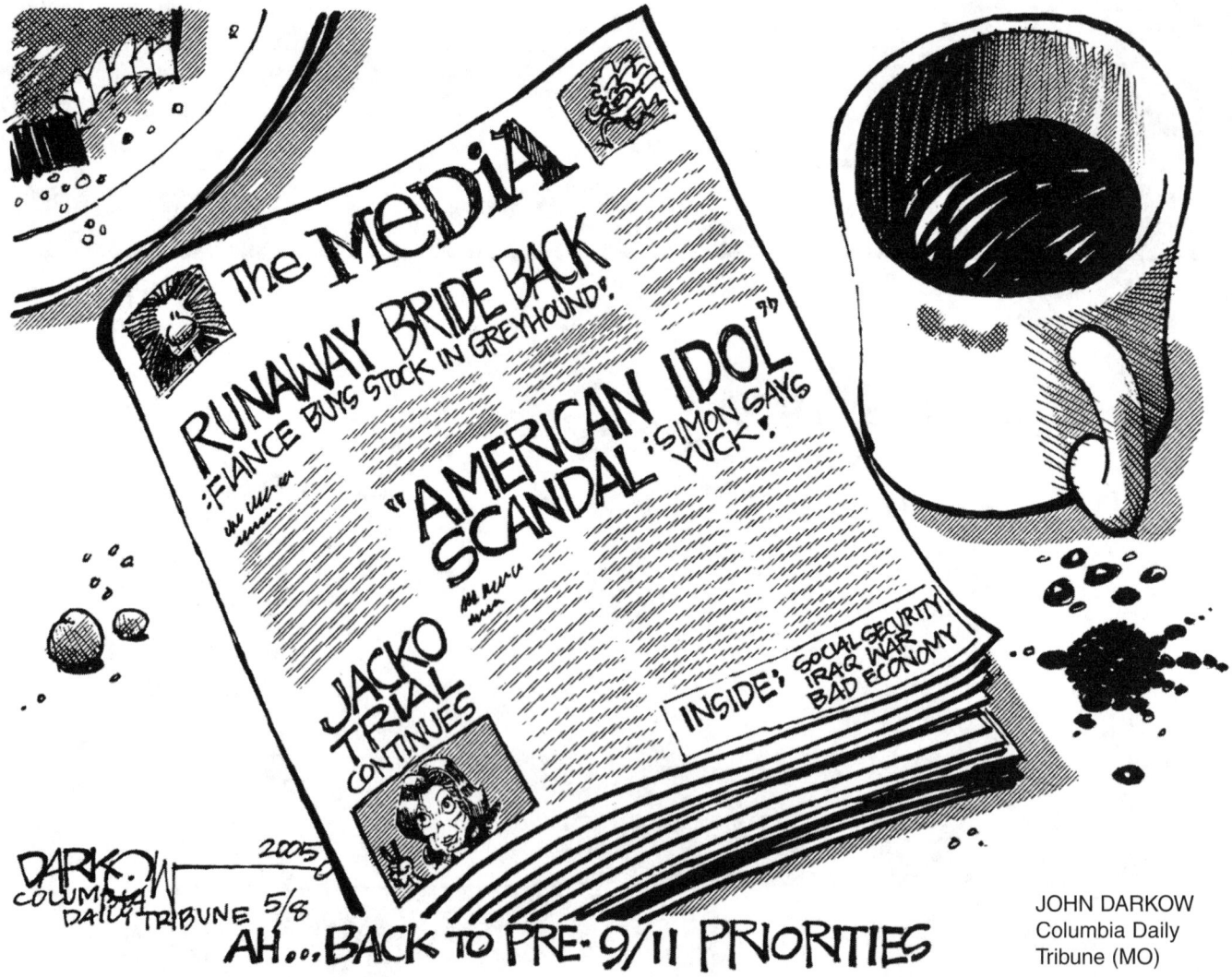

JOHN DARKOW
Columbia Daily
Tribune (MO)

R.J. MATSON
Roll Call

RUNAWAY BRIDE

"HELLO, POLICE? I'M SUPPOSED TO BE MARRIED TO THE PRESIDENT'S SOCIAL SECURITY PLAN... *BUT I'VE BEEN KIDNAPPED!*"

DAN WASSERMAN, Boston Globe

DANA SUMMERS, Orlando Sentinel

DATING TIP:
LEARN TO RECOGNIZE A RELATIONSHIP THAT MAY NOT BE WORTH PURSUING...

TUESDAY WON'T WORK EITHER — I'M PLANNING ON BEING KIDNAPPED THAT NIGHT, TOO...

PHYSICS

PAT BAGLEY, Salt Lake Tribune

CHRIS BRITT, State Journal-Register

JACK OHMAN, Portland Oregonian

RUNAWAY BRIDE

DWANE POWELL, Raleigh News & Observer

BOB GORRELL, Creators Syndicate

CLAY JONES
Freelance-Star (VA)

MIKE LESTER, Rome News-Tribune (GA)

GARY BROOKINS, Richmond Times-Dispatch

KEN CATALINO
Creators Syndicate

MIKE LANE
Cagle Cartoons

DICK LOCHER, Chicago Tribune

PATRICK O'CONNOR, Los Angeles Daily News

BILL SCHORR, AM New York

ROB ROGERS, Pittsburgh Post-Gazette

BRUCE PLANTE, Chattanooga Times Free Press

STEVE KELLEY, New Orleans Times Picayune

Baseball and Steroids

In March, baseball stars from Mark McGwire to Sammy Sosa were subpoenaed to congressional hearings about steroid use. Baltimore Orioles first baseman Rafael Palmeiro denied using performance-enhancing drugs at the time, but later tested positive for steroids, sparking a firestorm of criticism and cartoons. Slugger Barry Bonds was accused of using steroids, and claimed that he didn't know what he was using. The meaty athletes made meaty news, and cartoonists descended on the scandal like vultures on a fresh kill ... it was just that easy.

DARYL CAGLE
Slate.com

M.e. COHEN

R.J. MATSON, Roll Call

DICK LOCHER, Chicago Tribune

©2003 CHICAGO TRIBUNE
LOCHER
PALMEIRO

NATE BEELER, Washington Examiner

DICK WRIGHT, Copley News Service

STEVE BREEN, San Diego Union-Tribune

LARRY WRIGHT, Detroit News

PATRICK O'CONNOR, Los Angeles Daily News

BOB GORRELL, Creators Syndicate

MARSHALL RAMSEY, Clarion Ledger

JOE HELLER, Green Bay Press-Gazette

STEVE KELLEY, New Orleans Times Picayune

DANA SUMMERS, Orlando Sentinel

BRUCE PLANTE, Chattanooga Times Free

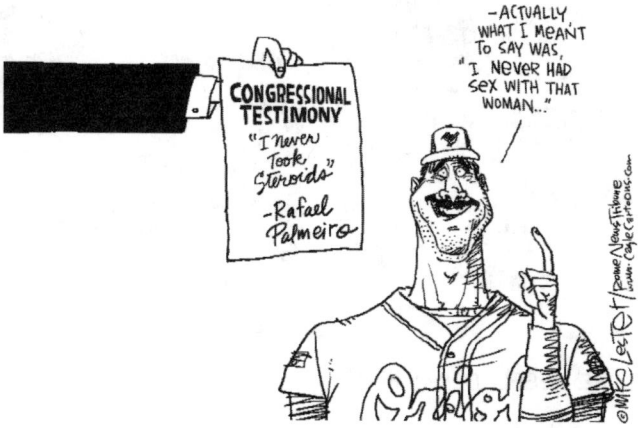

MIKE LESTER, Rome News-Tribune (GA)

DAVID CATROW, Springfield News-Sun

DICK LOCHER, Chicago Tribune

VIC HARVILLE, Stephens Media Group

MIKE KEEFE, Denver Post

MIKE KEEFE, Denver Post

WAYNE STAYSKAL, Tribune Media Services

STEVE NEASE, Oakville Beaver

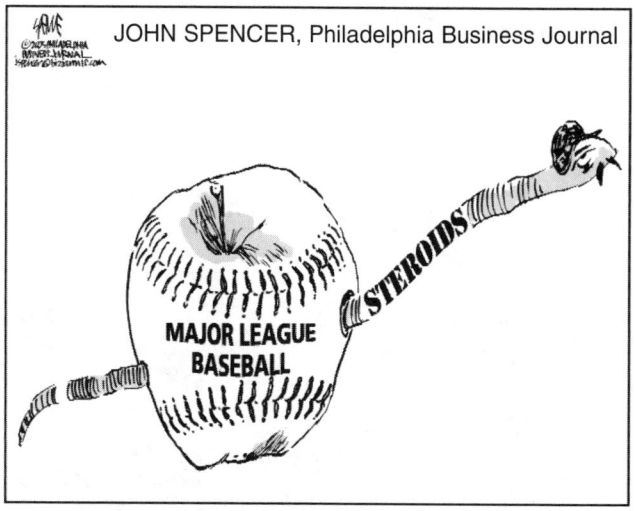

JOHN SPENCER, Philadelphia Business Journal

ARES, Cagle Cartoons

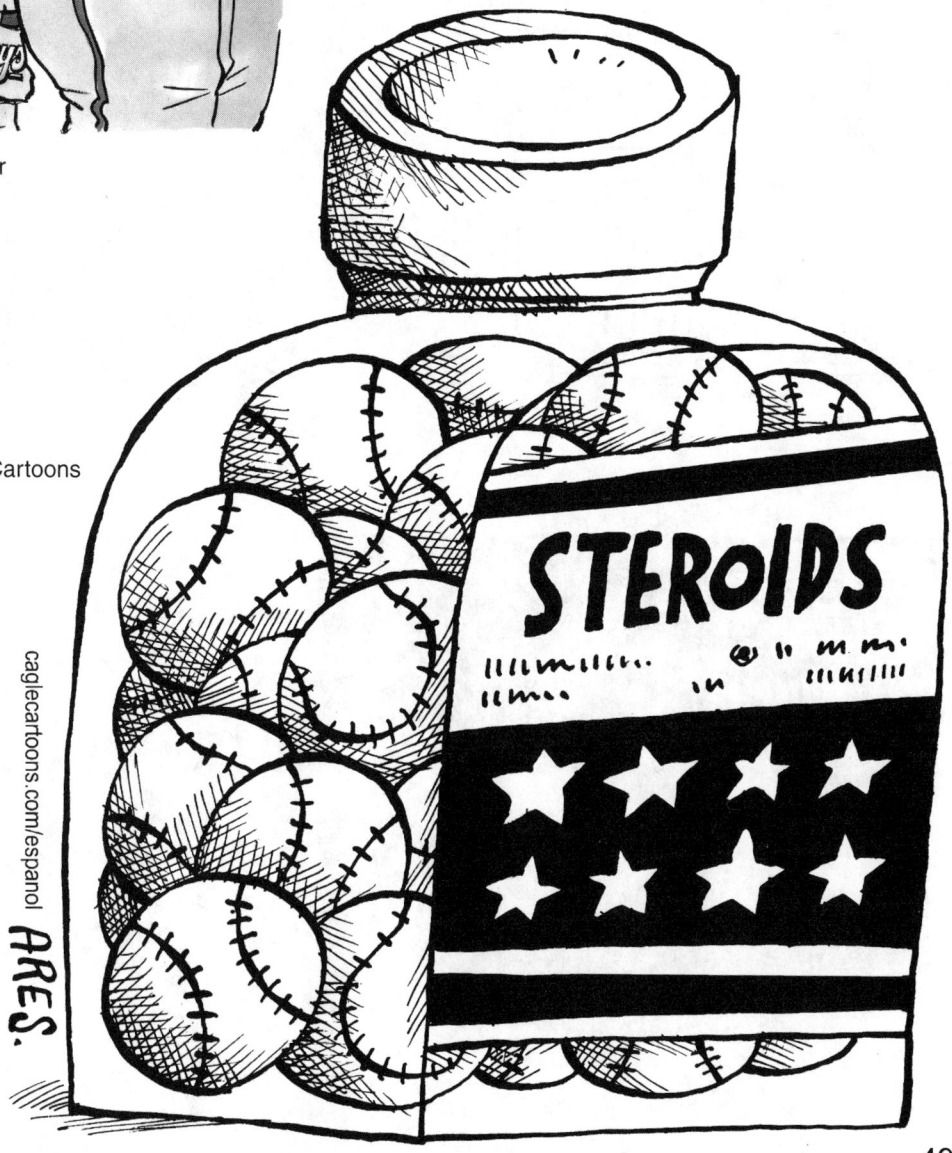

DARYL CAGLE, Slate.com

BRIAN FAIRRINGTON, Cagle Cartoons

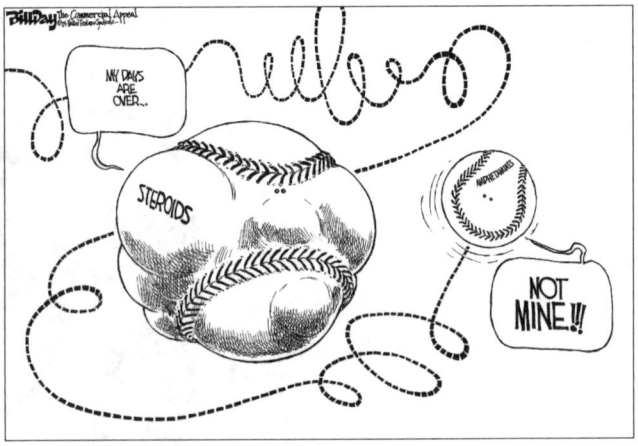

BILL DAY, Memphis Commercial Appeal

DARYL CAGLE, Slate.com

THE McGINTY FAMILY, WHICH LIVES NEXT DOOR TO THE BONDS FAMILY, ALSO HAD NO IDEA THAT CREAM WAS REALLY STEROIDS.

NATE BEELER, Washington Examiner

MIKE THOMPSON, Detroit Free-Press

CHUCK ASAY, Colorado Springs Gazette

CAMERON CARDOW, Ottawa Citizen

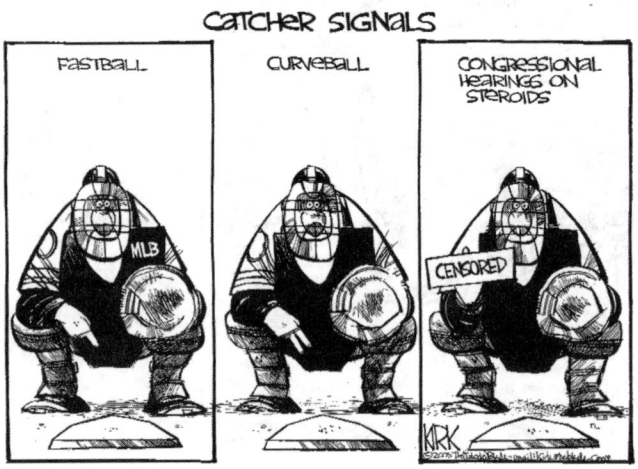

KIRK WALTERS, Toledo Blade

CHIP BOK, Akron Beacon-Journal

J.D. CROWE, Mobile Register

GARY BROOKINS, Richmond Times-Dispatch

CLAY JONES, Freelance-Star (VA)

BOB GORRELL, Creators Syndicate

PAUL COMBS, Tampa Tribune

MIKE LESTER, Rome News-Tribune (GA)

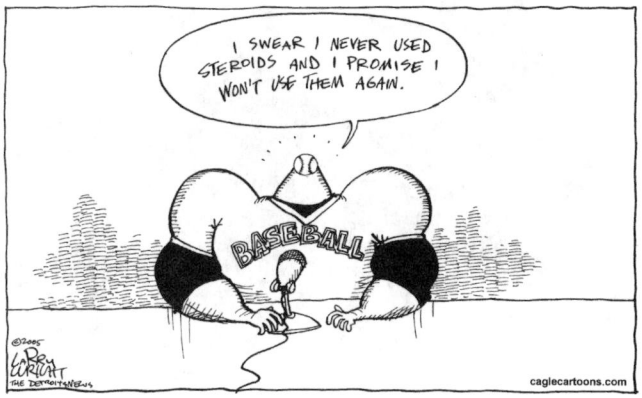

LARRY WRIGHT, Detroit News

JACK OHMAN, Portland Oregonian

DEERING ARKANSAS DEMOCRAT-GAZETTE
©2004 CREATORS SYNDICATE, INC.

...AND TODAY TODAY TODAY I CONSIDER MYSELF MYSELF MYSELF... THE LUCKIEST STEROID ABUSER ON THE FACE OF THE EARTH THE EARTH THE EARTH.....

BASEBALL

JOHN DEERING, Arkansas Democrat Gazette

MIKE LESTER, Rome News-Tribune (GA)

MILT PRIGGEE

ANDY SINGER, No Exit

MIKE LESTER, Rome News-Tribune (GA)

STEVE KELLEY, New Orleans Times Picayune

MIKE THOMPSON, Detroit Free-Press

LARRY WRIGHT, Detroit News

Michael Jackson Verdict

Michael Jackson was so relieved he was found not guilty in his trial for child molestation, he threw a star-studded party to celebrate. But cartoonists thought he looked so guilty that the verdict didn't really matter.

MIKE LESTER, Rome News-Tribune (GA)

BRIAN FAIRRINGTON, Cagle Cartoons

PAUL CONRAD
Tribune Media Services

"IF THE GLOVE WON'T FIT, YOU MUST ACQUIT!"

DOUG MARLETTE, Tallahassee Democrat

DANA SUMMERS
Orlando Sentinel

MICHAEL RAMIREZ
Los Angeles Times

BILL SCHORR, AM New York

PATRICK CHAPPATTE, International Herald Tribune

LALO ALCARAZ, L.A. Weekly

DAVID HORSEY, Seattle Post Intelligencer

STEVE KELLEY, New Orleans Times Picayune

J.D. CROWE, Mobile Register

STEVE NEASE, Oakville Beaver

WALT HANDELSMAN, Newsday

MICHAEL JACKSON, YOU'VE JUST BEEN ACQUITTED. WHAT ARE YOU GOING TO DO NOW?

STEVE BREEN, San Diego Union-Tribune

WAYNE STAYSKAL, Tribune Media Services

CHRIS BRITT, State Journal-Register

GRONDAHL
STANDARD-EXAMINER

NEVERLAND

BOY FOR SALE!

CALIFORNIA MAY NOW RETURN TO NORMAL

CAL GRONDAHL
Utah Standard Examiner

SIGNE WILKINSON
Philadelphia Daily News

JOE HELLER, Green Bay Press-Gazette

GARY BROOKINS, Richmond Times-Dispatch

VINCE O'FARRELL, Australia

SCOTT STANTIS, Birmingham News

STEVE BENSON, Arizona Republic

DAVID FITZSIMMONS, Arizona Daily Star

BRIAN ADCOCK, Scotland

NICK ANDERSON, Louisville Courier-Journal

DARYL CAGLE
Slate.com

WELL, BUBBLES, IT'S FINALLY OVER. THIS PROVES AT LAST I'M JUST A NORMAL GUY....

FORGET IT, FREAK. YOU STILL CAN'T SLEEP WITH MY KIDS....

MIKE RAMIREZ, Los Angeles Times

DARYL CAGLE
Slate.com

Back to where he came from...

THOMAS BOLDT, Calgary Sun

STEVE GREENBERG, Ventura County Star

JOHN COLE, Scranton Times-Tribune

STEVE SACK, Minneapolis Star-Tribune

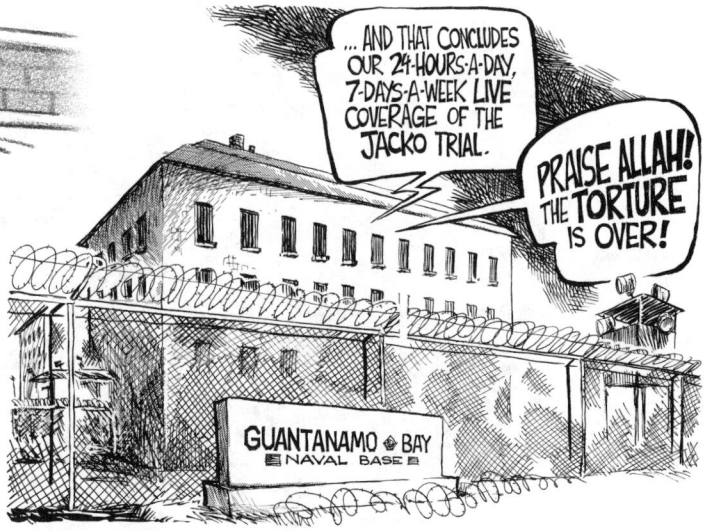

NATE BEELER
Washington Examiner

John Bolton

President Bush's nomination of John Bolton as U.S. Ambassador to the United Nations was met with protests from many Democrats and a few Republicans, and a filibuster in the Senate. More than two months into the debate, Bush installed Bolton without congressional approval through a "recess appointment" while Congress was on vacation. Bolton's bushy, white moustache was a gift to cartoonists.

STEVE SACK, Minneapolis Star-Tribune

PAUL CONRAD
Tribune Media Services

WILL THE REAL JOHN BOLTON PLEASE STAND UP?

R.J. MATSON
St. Louis Post Dispatch

SCARY ISN'T IT? JOHN BOLTON IS SET TO BECOME OUR NEW AMBASSADOR TO THE U.N.... ...TELL ME, WHAT IS IT WITH THE MUSTACHE?

THAT'S NO MUSTACHE... HE'S GOT A **PEACE DOVE** CLENCHED IN HIS TEETH...

caglecartoons.com

©2005 FLORIDA TODAY JEFF PARKER

JEFF PARKER, Florida Today

JOHN SHERFFIUS

"MY SENAD COLLEAGUES DESERVE AN UP OR DOWN VOTE WID DIS GUY."

PAT BAGLEY, Salt Lake Tribune

JOHN BOLTON

NATE BEELER
Washington Examiner

MONTE WOLVERTON, Cagle Cartoons

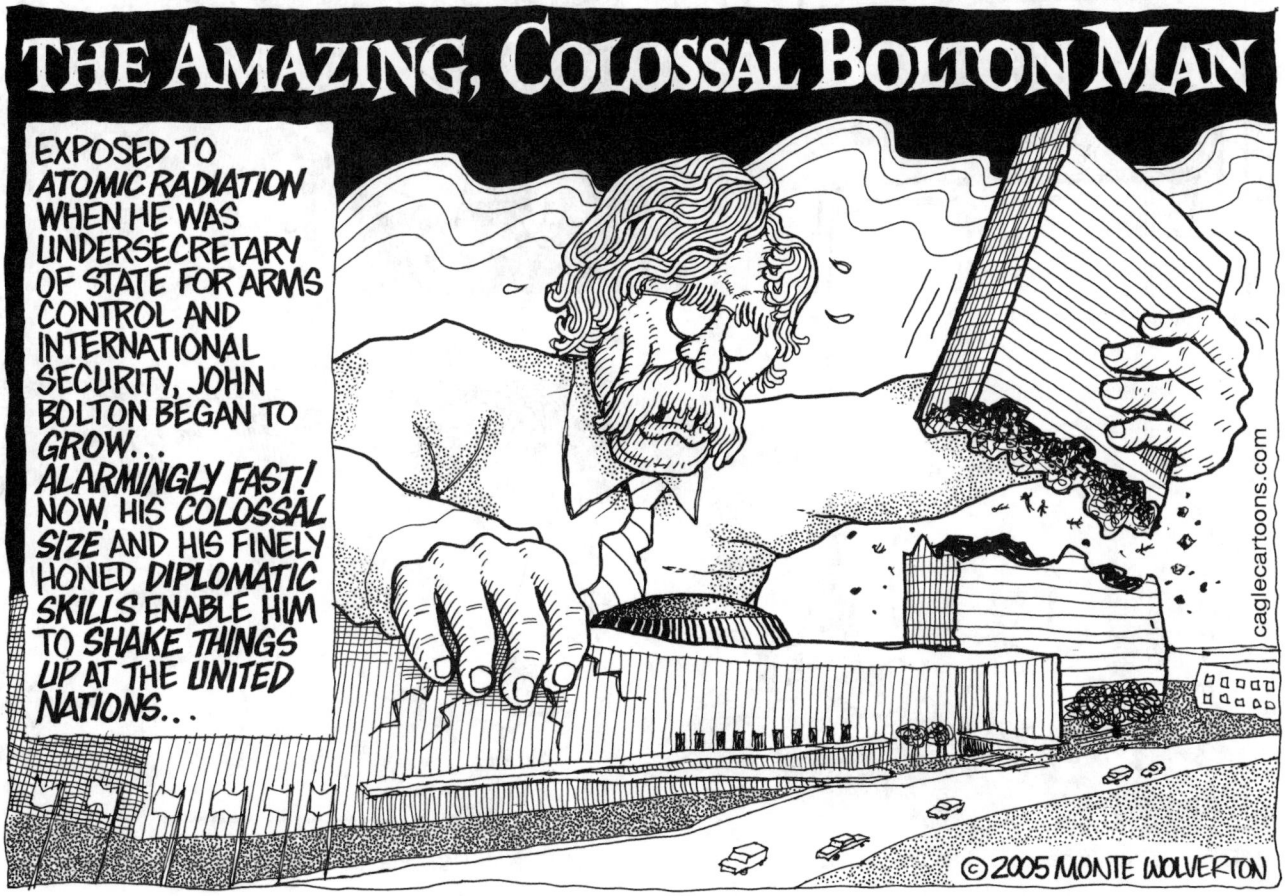

©2005 FLORIDA TODAY
caglecartoons.com
JEFF PARKER

HEEERE'S JOHNNY!!

U.N.

jparker@flatoday.net

JEFF PARKER, Florida Today

STEVE SACK, Minneapolis Star-Tribune

DANA SUMMERS, Orlando Sentinel

JOHN TREVER, Albuquerque Journal

ROB ROGERS, Pittsburgh Post-Gazette

STEVE GREENBERG, Ventura County Star

ED STEIN, Rocky Mountain News

MIKE KEEFE, Denver Post

MIKE LANE, Cagle Cartoons

BRUCE PLANTE, Chattanooga Times Free Press

CHIP BOK, Akron Beacon-Journal

ERIC ALLIE, Pioneer Press (IL)

MICHAEL RAMIREZ, Los Angeles Times

DREW SHENEMAN, Newark Star-Ledger

PAUL CONRAD, Tribune Media Services

MIKE THOMPSON, Detroit Free-Press

DARYL CAGLE
Slate.com

PATRICK O'CONNOR, Los Angeles Daily News

STEPHANE PERAY, Thailand

KEN CATALINO, National/Freelance

"We've been assigned to follow Bolton around if he's confirmed."

BRUCE BEATTIE, Daytona News-Journal

"JOHN BOLTON?!... AND LET THE ARROGANT, WAR-MONGERING, LYING, IMMORAL AMERICANS LOWER OUR LEVEL OF DISCOURSE?!"

BOB GORRELL, Creators Syndicate

DAVID HORSEY, Seattle Post Intelligencer

ROBERT ARIAIL, The State (SC)

CHUCK ASAY, Colorado Springs Gazette

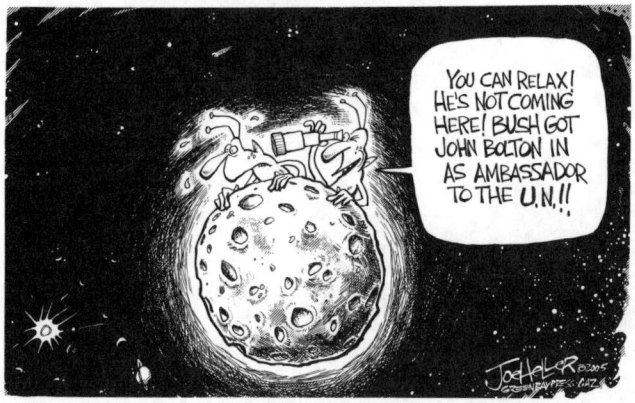

JOE HELLER, Green Bay Press-Gazette

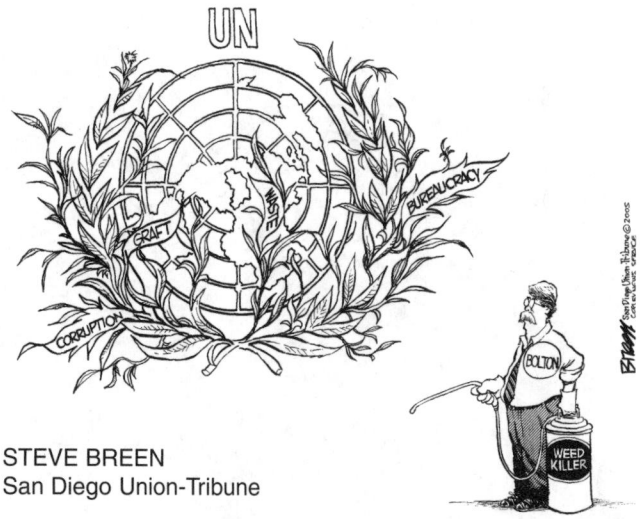

STEVE BREEN
San Diego Union-Tribune

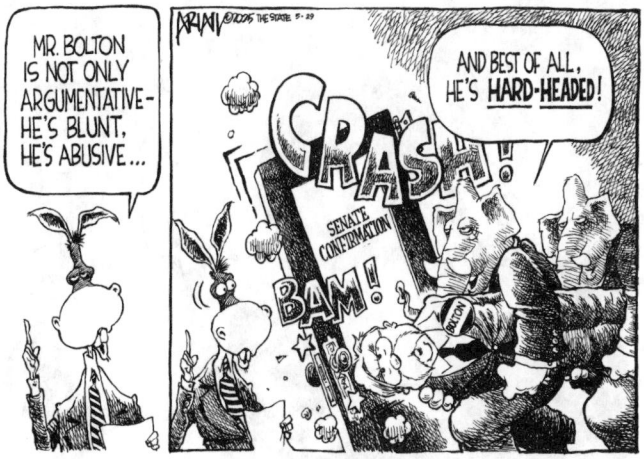

ROBERT ARIAIL, The State (SC)

MIKE MIKULA, Roll Call

Pope John Paul II & Pope Benedict XVI

Pope John Paul II, who was the third-longest-reigning pope in the history of the Roman Catholic Church, died on April 2. Two and a half weeks later, conservative Cardinal Joseph Ratzinger was elected Pope Benedict XVI, becoming the first German pope since 1523. Cartoonists mourned and memorialized Pope John Paul II, but most were critical of Ratzinger, a former member of the Hitler Youth and a soldier in the German army. Although membership in the Nazi organizations was mandatory at the time, cartoonists seized on Nazi Germany as a metaphor for the new pope's reputation as the defender of conservative orthodoxy in the church.

ARCADIO ESQUIVEL, Costa Rica

M.e. COHEN

TIM MENEES, Pittsburgh Post-Gazette

DOUG MARLETTE, Tribune Media Services

ANTONIO NERIL LICON, Mexico

CLAY BENNETT, Christian Science Monitor

DAVID FITZSIMMONS, Arizona Daily Star

STEPHANE PERAY, Thailand

JIMMY MARGULIES, The Record

VINCE O'FARRELL, Australia

DICK WRIGHT, Columbus Dispatch

MATT DAVIES, Journal News (NY)

JEFF PARKER
Florida Today

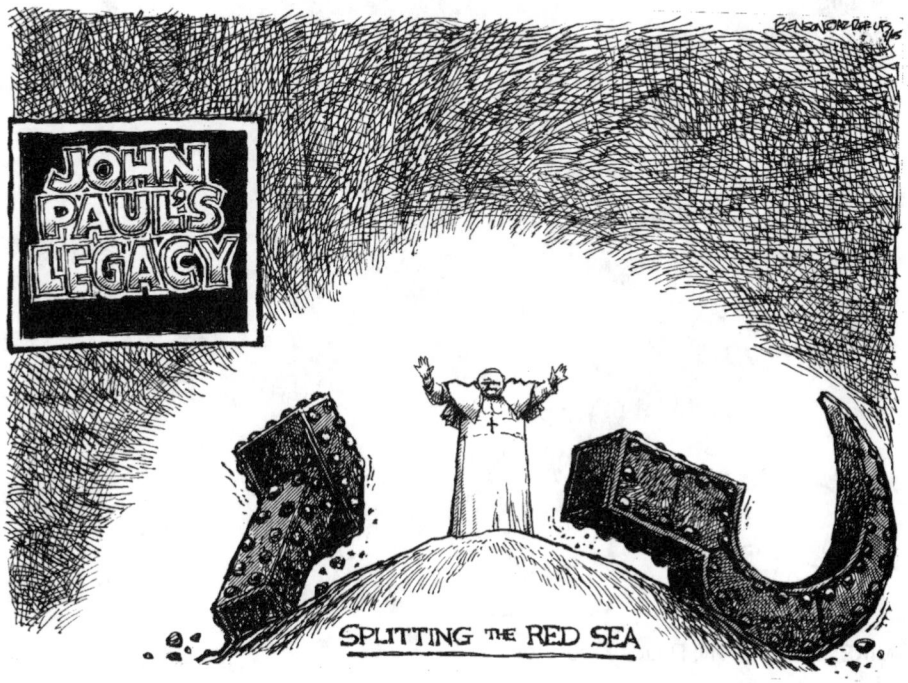

STEVE BENSON
Arizona Republic

WELCOME, EL PAPA, TO YOUR FINAL DESTINATION.

©2005 CHICAGO TRIBUNE

DICK LOCHER, Chicago Tribune

MIKE THOMPSON, Detroit Free-Press

HENRY PAYNE, Detroit News

OLD POPE, NEW POPE

SHERFFIUS ©4-1-05 jsherffius@aol.com

JOHN SHERFFIUS

THOMAS BOLDT, Calgary Sun

STEVE KELLEY, New Orleans Times Picayune

DARYL CAGLE, Slate.com

KIRK WALTERS, Toledo Blade

HENRY PAYNE, Detroit News

"POPE JOHN PAUL'S HALO."

OLD POPE, NEW POPE

GRAEME MACKAY, Hamilton Spectator

POPE JOHN PAUL II

MACKAY
HAMILTON SPECTATOR

www.caglecartoons.com/espanol

OSMANI SIMANCA
Brazil

NATE BEELER, Washington Examiner

KEN CATALINO, Creators Syndicate

PAT BAGLEY, Salt Lake Tribune

OLD POPE, NEW POPE

DARYL CAGLE
Slate.com

JIM DAY, Las Vegas Review Journal

OSMANI SIMANCA, Brazil
www.caglecartons.com/espanol
SIMANCA

ANTONIO NERIL LICON
Mexico

LAILSON de HOLLANDA
Brazil

SERGIO LANGER, Argentina

STEVE NEASE, Oakville Beaver

DAVID HORSEY, Seattle Post Intelligencer

DICK LOCHER, Chicago Tribune

THOMAS BOLDT, Calgary Sun

MIKE KEEFE, Denver Post

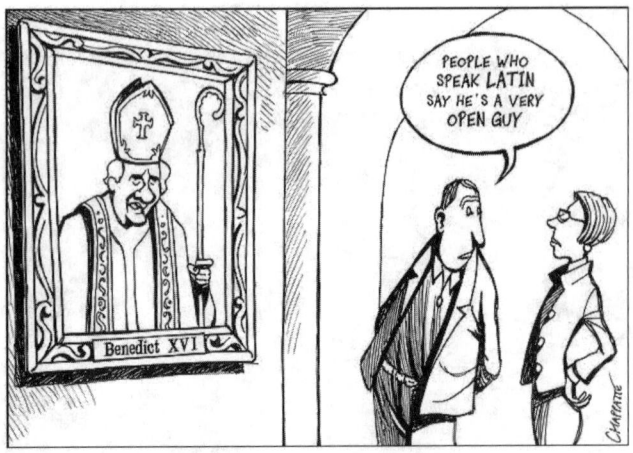

PATRICK CHAPPATTE, International Herald Tribune

PATRICK CHAPPATTE, International Herald

ARCADIO ESQUIVEL
Costa Rica

OSMANI SIMANCA, Brazil

HENRY PAYNE, Detroit News

STEVE SACK
Minneapolis Star-Tribune

JEFF PARKER, Florida Today

JEFF PARKER ©2005 FLORIDA TODAY
caglecartoons.com
...ON HIS LEFT WRIST?...THAT'S POPE BENEDICT'S "WHAT WOULD JOHN PAUL DO" BRACELET...
jparker@flatoday.net

Terri Schiavo

Conservatives went to unprecedented lengths to overrule Terri Schiavo's husband and the courts to pass federal legislation that would allow federal courts to consider reinsertion of her feeding tube. Schiavo had been in a persistent vegetative state for 15 years, unable to survive without a feeding tube and constant care. Republicans Sen. Bill Frist, Sen. Rick Santorum, and Rep.Tom DeLay were ultimately unsuccessful—Terri Schiavo died on March 31. The whole saga was full of crazy characters and impassioned accusations.

OSMANI SIMANCA, Brazil

DARYL CAGLE
Slate.com

R.J. MATSON
Roll Call

"WE'LL PAY EXTRA IF YOU CAN WORD IT SO IT'S A FEDERAL CRIME FOR ANY POLITICIAN TO EXPLOIT OUR INCAPACITATION"

MIKE LESTER
Rome News-Tribune (GA)

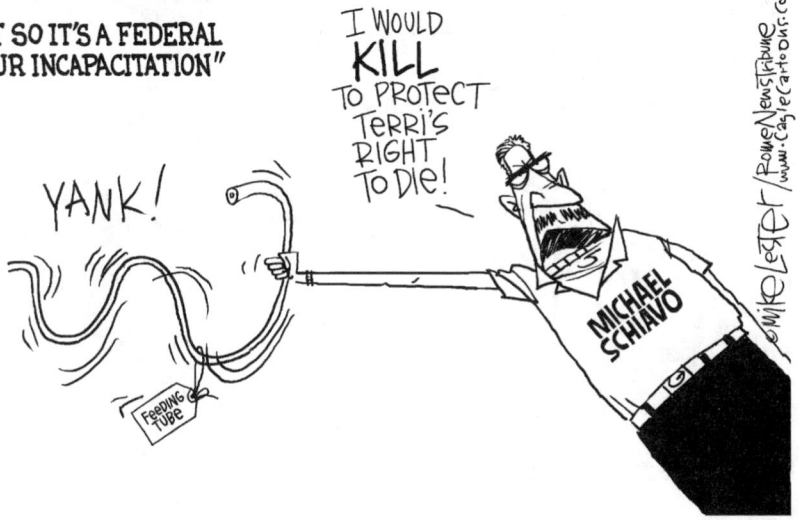

JONATHAN BROWN, Deseret News

MATT DAVIES, Journal News (NY)

CHUCK ASAY, Colorado Springs Gazette

DARYL CAGLE
Slate.com

CLAY BENNETT, Christian Science Monitor

CLAY BENNETT, Christian Science Monitor

'Don't tell me...You're here about a living will.'

MIKE LANE, Cagle Cartoons

MIKE LANE, Cagle Cartoons

MIKE LESTER
Rome News-Tribune (GA)

MIKE LESTER
Rome News-Tribune (GA)

DARYL CAGLE
Slate.com

TIM MENEES, Pittsburgh Post-Gazette

VINCE O'FARRELL, Cagle Cartoons

ROB ROGERS, Pittsburgh Post-Gazette

BRIAN FAIRRINGTON
Cagle Cartoons

PANDORA'S BOX
CAMERON CARDOW, Ottawa Citizen

SANDY HUFFAKER, National

PAUL COMBS, Tampa Tribune

STEVE SACK, Minneapolis Star-Tribune

MIKE THOMPSON, Detroit Free-Press

MIKE RAMIREZ
Los Angeles Times

THOMAS BOLDT, Calgary Sun

caglecartoon.com
tabtoons@telus.net

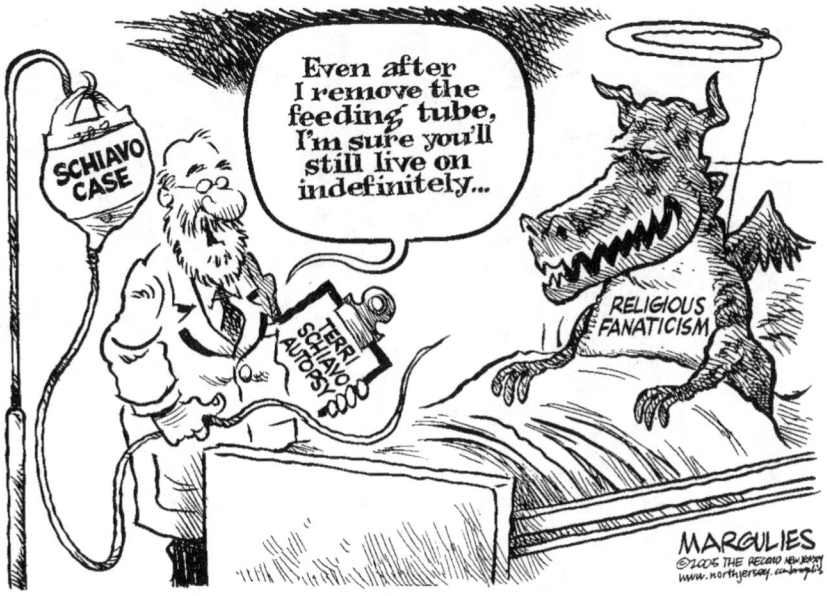

JIMMY MARGULIES
The Record

ERIC ALLIE, Pioneer Press (IL)

VIC HARVILLE, Stephens Media Group

GARY VARVEL, Indianapolis Star

BILL SCHORR, National Syndicated

DANA SUMMERS, Orlando Sentinel

PAUL COMBS, Tampa Tribune

BRUCE PLANTE, Chattanooga Times Free Press

STEVE GREENBERG, Ventura County Star

JOE HELLER, Green Bay Press-Gazette

Space Shuttle

When the first NASA space shuttle since the 2003 Columbia disaster took flight this year, many Americans held their breath. The shuttle Discovery, first flown in 1984, had problems before, during, and after takeoff that highlighted just how old NASA's technology was. America waited anxiously as an astronaut performed a spacewalk to inspect and repair a piece of material between tiles under the nose of the shuttle.

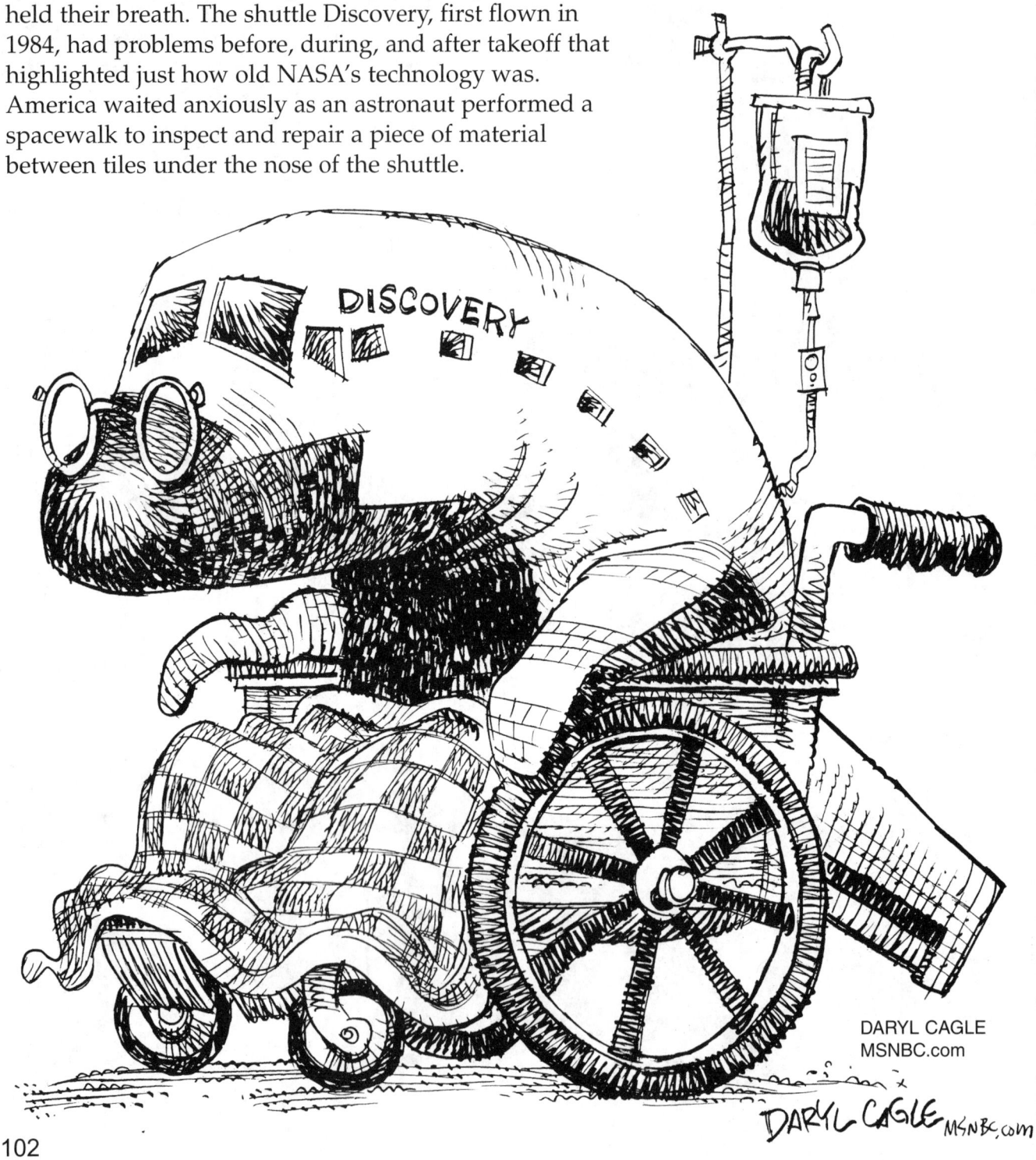

GARY VARVEL, Indianapolis Star

STEVE SACK, Minneapolis Star-Tribune

MIKE THOMPSON, Detroit Free-Press

IN PREPARATION OF A MARCH 2006 LAUNCH, NASA ANNOUNCES THAT IT HAS RECEIVED FEDERAL FUNDING FOR THE REPLACEMENT OF THE SHUTTLE'S VICTROLA WITH A BRAND NEW STATE OF THE ART 8-TRACK PLAYER.

DWAYNE BOOTH, Mr. Fish

JEFF KOTERBA, Omaha World Herald

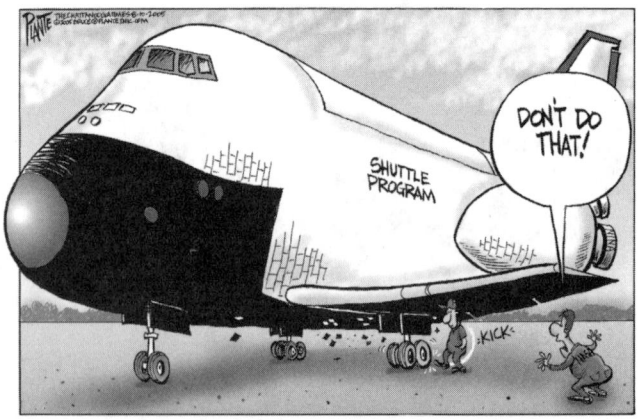

BRUCE PLANTE, Chattanooga Times Free Press

CAMERON CARDOW, Ottawa Citizen

CHIP BOK, Akron Beacon-Journal

DOUG MARLETTE, Tallahassee Democrat

JOE HELLER, Green Bay Press-Gazette

STEVE BENSON, Arizona Republic

MARSHALL RAMSEY, Clarion Ledger

BILLY DREAMING OF GROWING UP AND BECOMING TERRIFICALLY OUTDATED, PHILOSOPHICALLY MEANDERING, RIDICULOUSLY UNRELIABLE, BALL BREAKINGLY EXPENSIVE, AND BONE CRUSHINGLY BORING AND UNPOPULAR WITH THE AMERICAN PUBLIC.

DWAYNE BOOTH
Mr. Fish

J.D. CROWE, Mobile Register

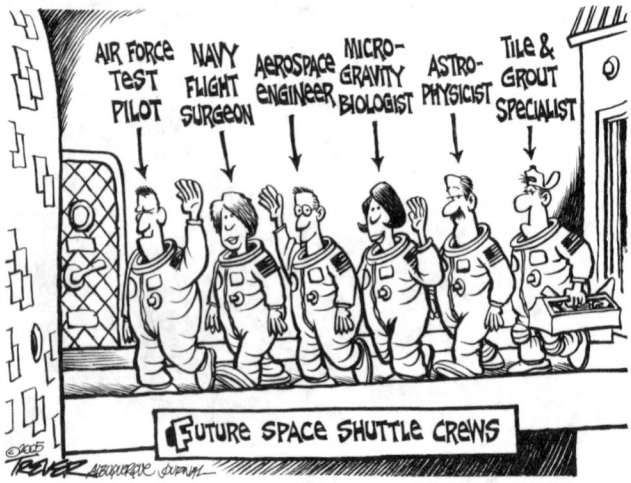

JOHN TREVER, Albuquerque Journal

"I TOOK A GREAT FALL... THEY PUT ME BACK TOGETHER... NOW THEY'RE TELLING ME I HAVE GAP FILLER ISSUES."

HENRY PAYNE, Detroit News

JEFF PARKER, Florida Today

MIKE GRASTON Windsor Star

SCOTT STANTIS, Birmingham News

"NO ONE EVER MENTIONS ALL THE STUFF THAT DIDN'T FALL OFF."

DREW SHENEMAN, Newark Star-Ledger

REX BABIN, Sacramento Bee

STEVE NEASE
Oakville Beaver

WAITING TO EXHALE
JEFF PARKER, Florida Today

WAITER, THERE'S A SPACE SHUTTLE TILE IN MY SOUP...

NASA

ONE HOUR PARKING

©Mike Lester Rome News Tribune www.CagleCartoons.com

MIKE LESTER, Rome News-Tribune (GA)

DANA SUMMERS, Orlando Sentinel

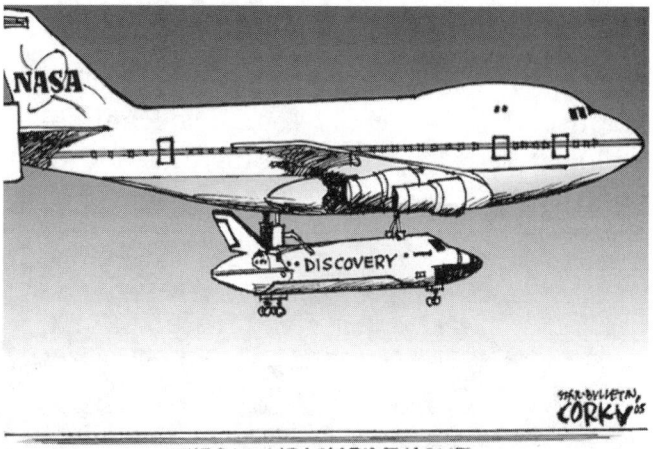

THE PIGGYBACK RIDE HOME...

CORKY TRINIDAD, Honolulu Star Bulletin

GRAEME MACKAY, Hamilton Spectator

Tom DeLay

House Majority Leader Tom "The Hammer" DeLay was big news in 2005. He campaigned to reinsert Terri Schiavo's feeding tube and then chastised the Supreme Court when they refused to hear the case: "There will come a time for the men responsible for this to answer for their behavior," DeLay said. Allegations surfaced that he misused federal investigative agencies to bring Democratic representatives back to Texas when they fled to avoid DeLay's gerrymandering plans. DeLay was also accused of receiving numerous gifts and favors from indicted lobbyist Jack Abramoff. DeLay had to give up his majority leader position when he was indicted for violating a Texas state fundraising law.

TAYLOR JONES
Tribune Media Services

STEVE SACK
Minneapolis Star-Tribune

JOHN BRANCH, San Antonio Express-News

REX BABIN, Sacramento Bee

DICK WRIGHT, Columbus Dispatch

DARYL CAGLE
Slate.com

STEVE SACK
Minneapolis Star-Tribune

TOM DELAY

CHIP BOK, Akron Beacon-Journal

NATE BEELER, Washington Examiner

MATT DAVIES, Journal News (NY)

M.e. COHEN

JIM DAY, Las Vegas Review Journal

CHUCK ASAY
Colorado Springs
Gazette

TOM DELAY

REX BABIN
Sacramento Bee

DAVID HORSEY
Seattle Post Intelligencer

ETTA HULME
Ft. Worth Star Telegram

MARK STREETER
Savannah Morning News

ERIC DEVERICKS
Seattle Times

DARYL CAGLE
MSNBC.com

SIGNE WILKINSON, Philadelphia Daily News

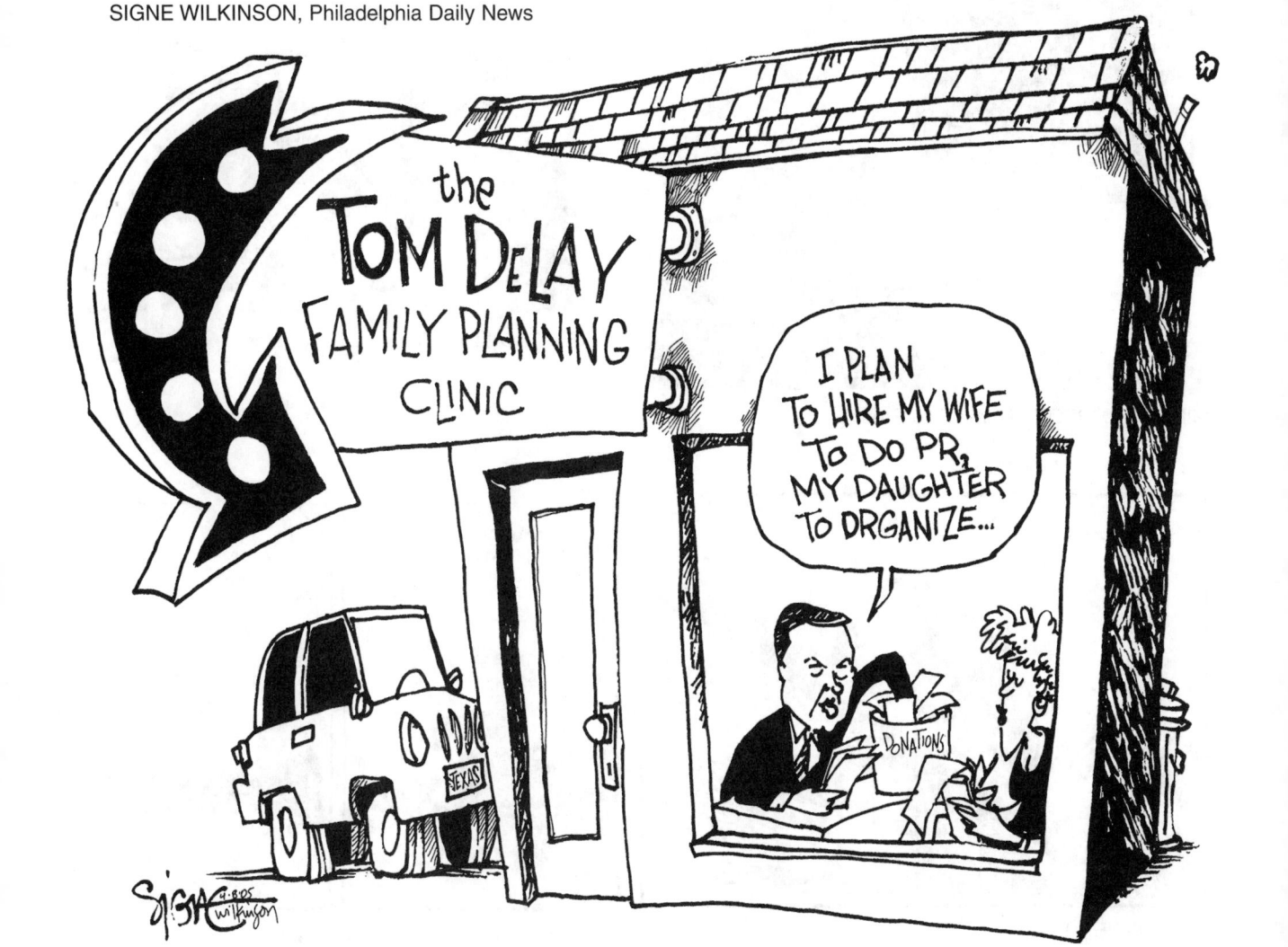

NATE BEELER
Washington Examiner

MIKE THOMPSON, Detroit Free-Press

KEN CATALINO, Creators Syndicate

J.D. CROWE, Mobile Register

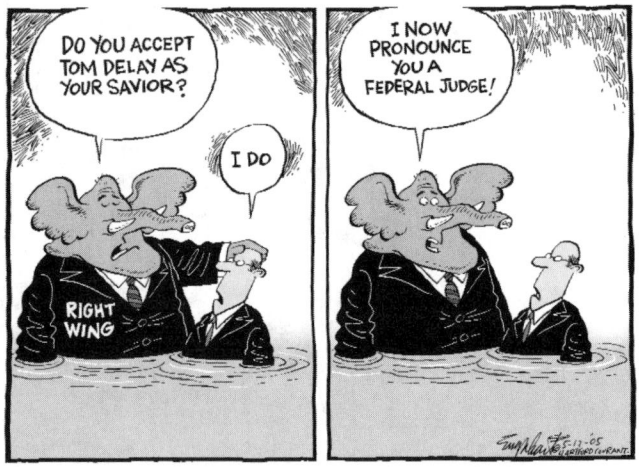

BOB ENGLEHART, Hartford Courant

MIKE LANE, Cagle Cartoons

MILT PRIGGEE

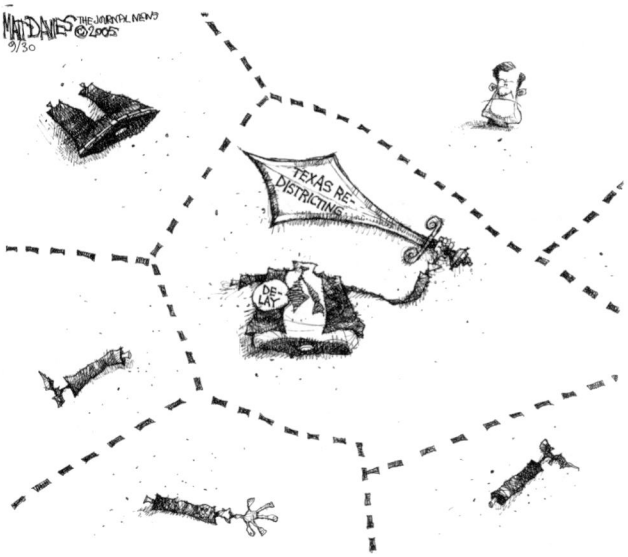

MATT DAVIES, Journal News (NY)

JIMMY MARGULIES, The Record (NJ)

TOM DeLAY'S DAY PLANNER

DREW SHENEMAN, Newark Star-Ledger

MONTE WOLVERTON, Cagle Cartoons

MARK STREETER, Savannah Morning News

JOHN TREVER, Albuquerque Journal

Minutemen

Illegal immigrants (or "undocumented workers") flooded into the United States again this year as a group of self-appointed vigilantes (or "patriots") who called themselves the "Minutemen" patrolled the borders in the Southwest. Politicians debated what entitlements should be given to illegal/undocumented immigrants, from driver's licenses to in-state tuition fees at universities.

BRIAN FAIRRINGTON, Cagle Cartoons

REX BABIN, Sacramento Bee

MIKE RAMIREZ, Los Angeles Times

SCOTT STANTIS, Birmingham News

ANTONIO NERIL LICON, Mexico

DICK LOCHER, Chicago Tribune

GARY MARKSTEIN, Copley News Service

STEVE BREEN
San Diego Union Tribune

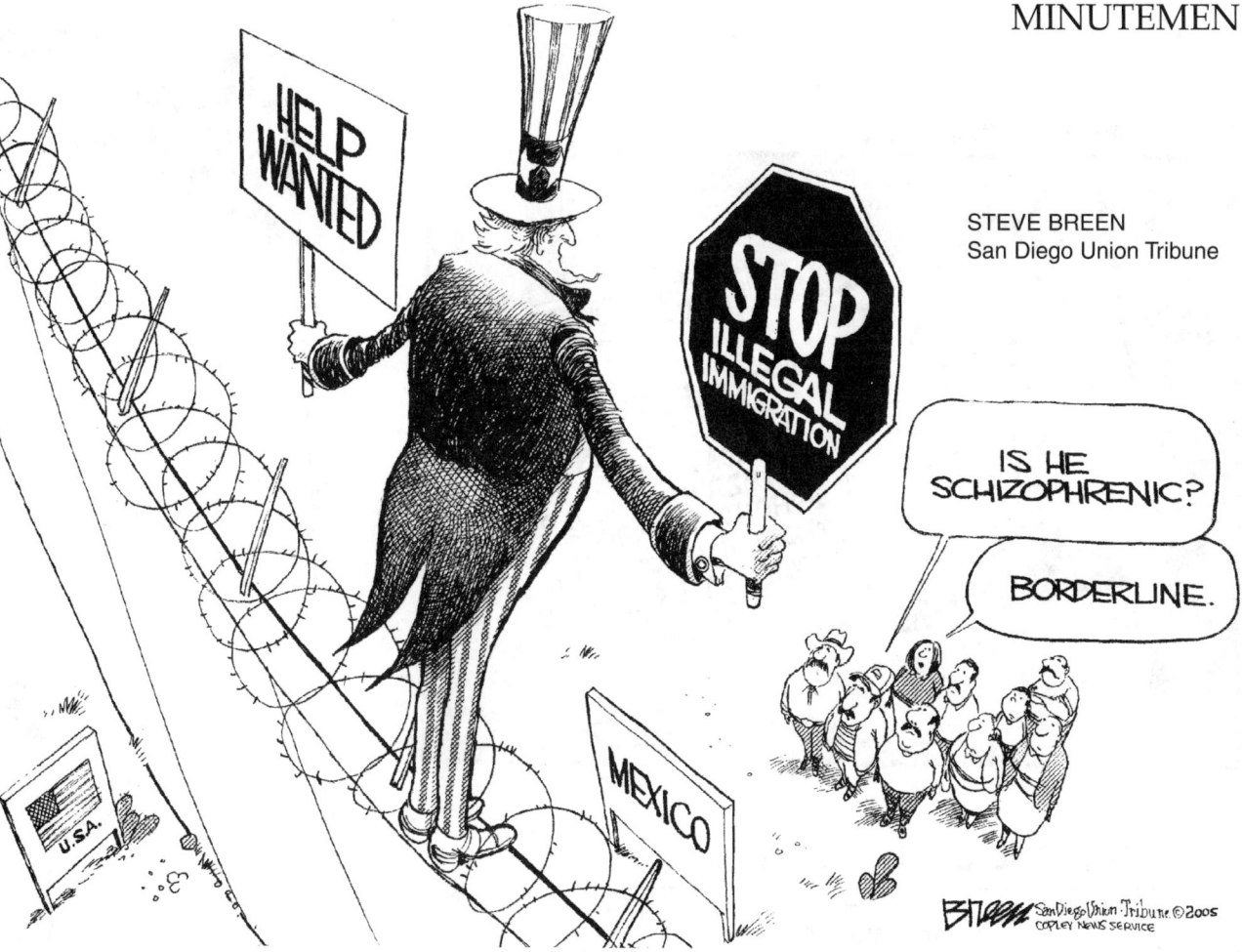

MIKE KEEFE
Denver Post

BOB ENGLEHART, Hartford Courant

ANDY SINGER, No Exit

bolicartoons.com/espanol

ANGEL BOLIGAN
Mexico

JOHN BRANCH, San Antonio Express-News

MIKE KEEFE, Denver Post

JOHN TREVER, Albuquerque Journal

London Bombing

On July 7, four home-grown, al-Qaeda suicide bombers hit London's public transportation during the morning rush hour, killing 56 and injuring 700. Two weeks later, another round of four explosions took place, again on the Underground and a public bus, but this time the bombs malfunctioned and no one was hurt. London was badly shaken by the deadliest act of terrorism in the U.K. since the 1988 bombing of Pan Am Flight 103. Cartoonists paid tribute to the casualties while reminding the world that terrorism wouldn't be going away anytime soon.

ANGEL BOLIGAN
Mexico

caglecartoons.com
tabstoons@telus.net

THOMAS BOLDT, Calgary Sun

PAUL COMBS, Tampa Tribune

PETAR PISMESTROVIC, Austria

JEFF PARKER
Florida Today

STEVE BREEN, San Diego Union Tribune

STEVE BENSON, Arizona Republic

STEVE NEASE, Oakville Beaver

CLAY BENNETT, Christian Science Monitor

LONDON BOMBING

BILL SCHORR
AM New York

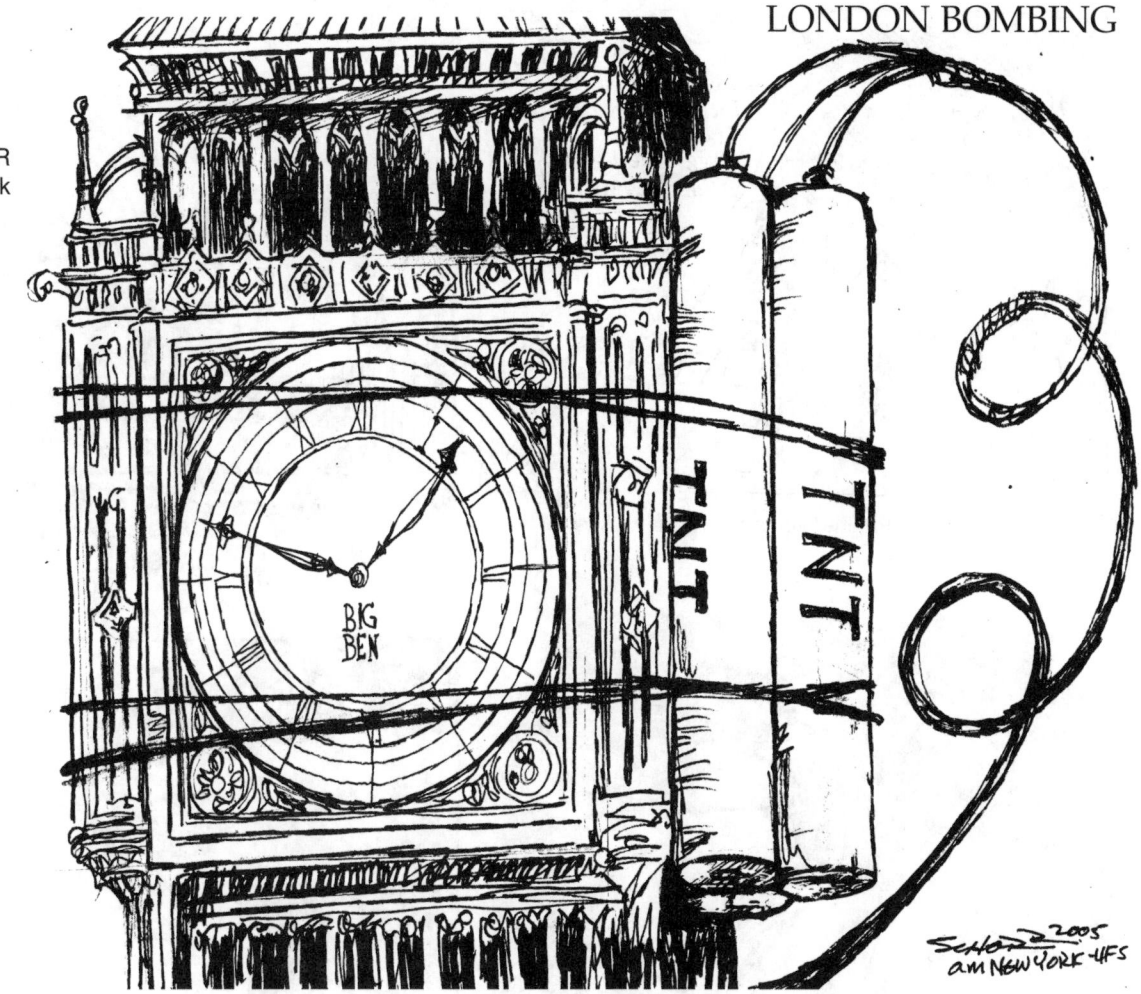

DARYL CAGLE
Slate.com

WAYNE STAYSKAL, Tribune Media Services

MARSHALL RAMSEY, Clarion Ledger

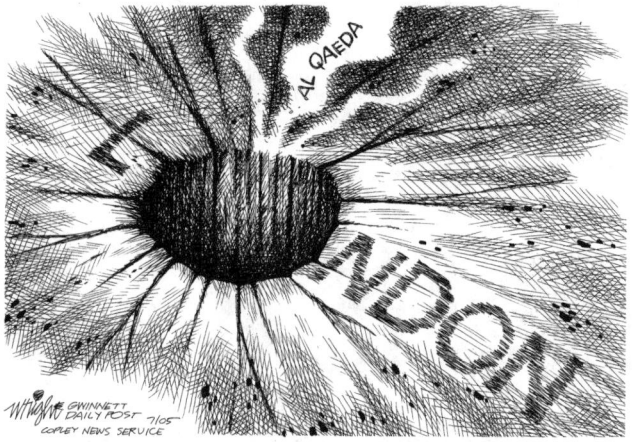

DICK WRIGHT, Copley News Service

TIM MENEES, Pittsburgh Post-Gazette

ADAM ZYGLIS, Buffalo News

WALT HANDELSMAN, Newsday

©MIKE LESTER / Rome News Tribune
www.caglecartoons.com

DID YOU NO HEAR ME, LAD? I SAID, GIMME' YOUR WALLET UNLESS YOU WANNA' DIE...

UNDERGROUND

Tick
Tick
Tick
Tick
Tick

MIKE LESTER, Rome News-Tribune (GA)

BROOKINS RICHMOND TIMES-DISPATCH 7/05

GARY BROOKINS
Richmond Times-Dispatch

JEFF KOTERBA
Omaha World Herald

TOWERS OF LONDON

PETER LEWIS
Australia

DREW SHENEMAN, Newark Star Ledger

OSMANI SIMANCA
Brazil

ALEN
LAUZAN
FALCON
Chile

RICHARD CROWSON
Witchita Eagle

EMAD HAJJAJ
Jordan

BRIAN ADCOCK, Scotland

CAMERON CARDOW
Ottawa Citizen

THE NEW LONDON MASS TRANSIT SYSTEM.

CHRISTO KOMARNITSKI, Bulgaria

BRIAN ADCOCK, Scotland

STEPHANE PERAY
Thailand

BRIAN ADCOCK
Scotland

THOMAS BOLDT, Calgary Sun

STEPHANE PERAY
Thailand

STEPHANE PERAY
Thailand

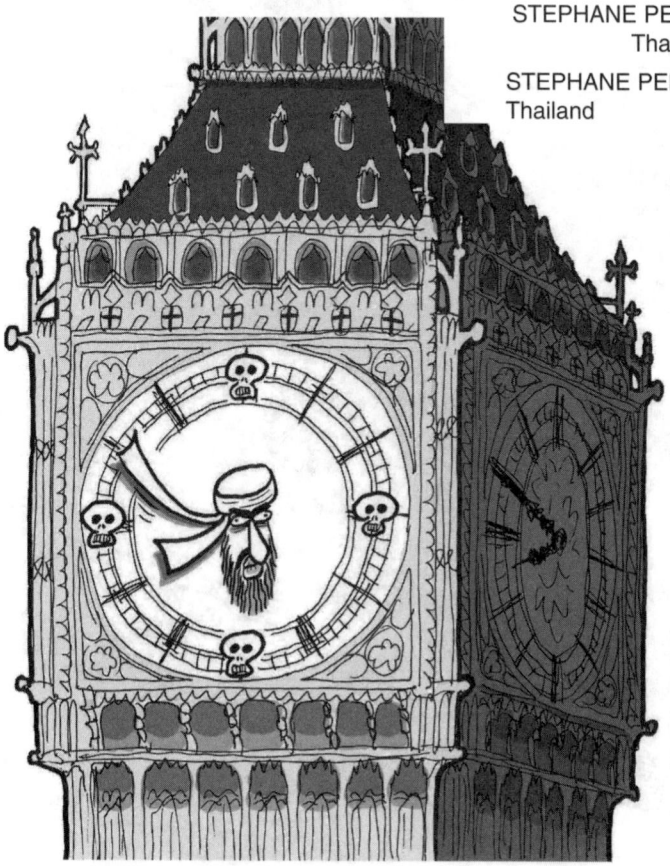

RANDY BISH, Pittsburgh Tribune Review

Pat Robertson

Television evangelist Pat Robertson called for the assassination of leftist Venezuelan President Hugo Chavez, yet another in a long line of goofy public statements to come from this "man of God."

TAYLOR JONES
Tribune Media Services

JEFF PARKER
Florida Today

BOB GORRELL
Creators Syndicate

DANA SUMMERS, Orlando Sentinel

STEVE BREEN, San Diego Union-Tribune

DAVID HORSEY, Seattle Post Intelligencer

JOE HELLER, Green Bay Press-Gazette

STEVE KELLEY, New Orleans Times Picayune

JACK OHMAN, Portland Oregonian

GARY MARKSTEIN, Copley News Service

CHIP BOK, Akron Beacon-Journal

CHRISTO KOMARNITSKI, Bulgaria

CLAY JONES, Freelance-Star (VA)

CAMERON CARDOW, Ottawa Citizen

BY GEORGE STEPHANOPOULOS

NATIONAL AFFAIRS

Why We Should Kill Saddam

The Iraqi leader isn't going away. That makes assassination may be Clinton's best option—if only he'd talk about it. BY GEORGE STEPHANOPOULOS

IN THE MIDDLE OF A CRISIS WITH IRAQ DURING FEBRUARY Clinton's first year, I actually sat down (I don't lie) with my staff to ponder the prospects of killing Saddam Hussein. Before I could finish the sentence, the then national security adviser Tony Lake looked up in the light fixtures and said "He was just kidding. We've not planning anything like that." Of all the words you just can't say in the modern White House, like "shred this," none is more taboo than "assassination."

Forgiveness. Most of our cold war efforts to kill foreign leaders like Fidel Castro (we planned to use exploding cigars and poisoned scuba suits) bordered on the criminal—and rarely worked. So in the wake of the Church Committee's revelation of CIA abuse in places like Cuba, Chile and the Congo, President Ford signed a sweeping, one-sentence executive order: "No person employed by or acting on behalf of the United States government shall engage in, or conspire to engage in, assassination."

But what's unlawful—and tragic—pile with the allies—is not necessarily immoral. So now that I'm out in the White House, I can say what I couldn't say then: we should seriously explore the assassination option. Even though the current crisis may be subsiding (on paper), we don't know what the future holds. A direct attack on Saddam would no doubt be politically risky—the president, concerned about his place in history, would be torn between the desire to get rid of a bully and the worry that an assassination plot gone awry would embarrass him late in his term. But the president should think about it the good war makes it festering, and we have not eliminated Saddam's capacity to inflict mass destruction. That's why killing him may be the most sensible—and moral—course over the long run.

Philosophers have long argued that there are times when murdering a murderer is not only necessary but noble. "Caesar is thought the bearer of the gods to those men who love their tyrants," wrote Cicero. Targeting Saddam also seems in accord with the "just war" principles first developed by Augustine and Aquinas. We've exhausted other efforts to stop him, and killing him certainly seems more proportionate to his crimes and discriminate in its effect than massive bombing raids that will too readily kill innocent civilians. To those who argue that assassination is the moral equivalent of terrorism, Michael Walzer's "Just and Unjust Wars" reminds us that "randomness is the crucial feature of terrorist activity." Even when kill the innocent to remove the powerful, Assassination, by contrast, is the least random act of war. Reducing the moral norm against it is a step established just if allowing it to go on unchecked with scoundrels like Saddam allow it to grow in his capacity to inflict WMD on his neighbors and the rest of the world. It's one of the few things we can do that will make us safer.

But can we do it? Another hand of just one decay is that the act of war must have a reasonable prospect of success. Here's where the assassination option gets trickier, though the legal prohibition is not as far as it appears at first glare—an executive order has the force of law, but it's essentially an obligation on a president (access on himself. If Clinton decides we can and should assassinate Saddam, he could call in national security adviser Sandy Berger and sign a secret National Security Decision Directive authorizing it.

The president would no doubt pay a heavy political price if the operation failed, but he would be a huge winner if it succeeded.

Overcoming the practical difficulties is much more problematic. Experts like former CIA director Robert Gates have said that assassination is a "necessity" because Saddam is so elusive and well protected. That's far, at least arguments against assassination, the it have some force when stacked against the alternatives, as indefinite extension of the sanctions that punisher the most vulnerable Iraqis without weakening Saddam or threatening his ability to build weapons of mass destruction; or a sure wave military campaign that will crack the gulf war coalition, risk allied troops and kill innocent Iraqis without snaring Saddam's hide.

So what could the president's choices be authorized? First, we could offer to provide money and material to Iraqi exiles willing to lead an effort to overthrow Saddam. (We tried this in the first term and it didn't work—but we should try again.) The second option is a covert plot to be carried out by the forces of Saddam's most likely to be lashed. President Reagan came close when he authorized this type of attack against Libya's Moammar Kadhafi. Though Saddam is even more difficult to track, we shouldn't pass up this opportunity if presented with reliable information on his whereabouts. But the third option is a side job: making contact with military leaders who are willing to risk killing massive two-dollar coups bands. This scenario carries the most risk for those involved—recent history shows that Saddam murdered for misinformation—and there is no guarantee that the new Iraqi president won't be another Saddam. If someone came forward, however, we should seriously weigh his direct help.

A misreading of the law or a judgment round representatives should not stop the president from talking about assassination. It should order up the options and see if it's possible. If we can kill Saddam, we should.

THOMAS STEPHANOPOULOS, former senior advisor to the president, is a Newsweek contributor.

NEWSWEEK DECEMBER 1, 1997

MIKE LESTER
Rome News-Tribune (GA)

PAT BAGLEY, Salt Lake Tribune

RICHARD CROWSON, Witchita Eagle

VIC HARVILLE, Stephens Media Group

DARYL CAGLE, MSNBC.com

MIKE RAMIREZ, Los Angeles Times

SANDY HUFFAKER, Cagle Cartoons

PAT ROBERTSON

CHRIS BRITT
State Journal Register (IL)

STEVE BENSON
Arizona Republic

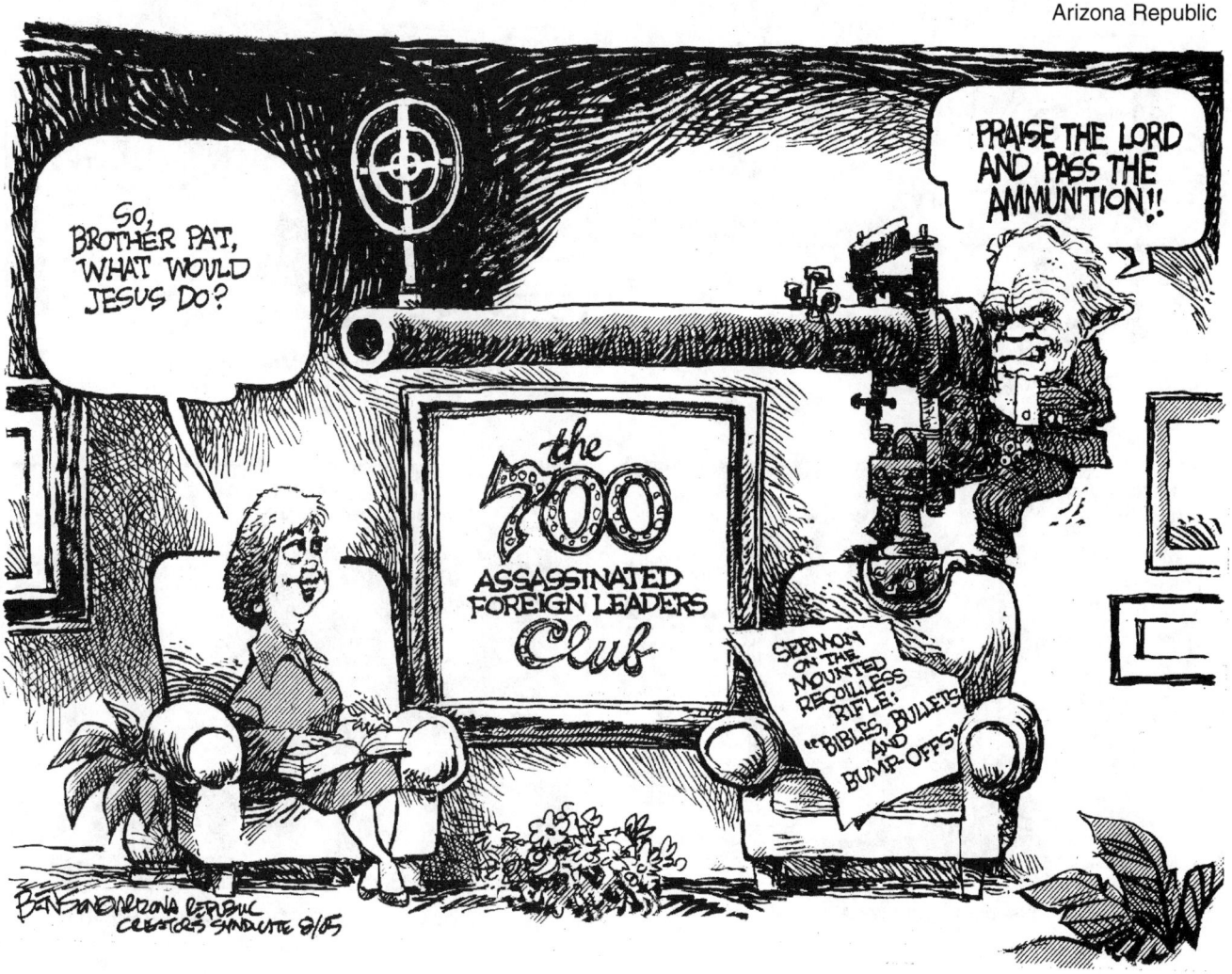

MICHAEL DEADDER, Halifax Daily News

CORKY TRINIDAD, Honolulu Star Bulletin

"THE FUNDAMENTALIST AMERICAN RELIGIOUS NUTS ARE STEALING OUR BEST LINES!"

HENRY PAYNE, Detroit News

MARK STREETER, Savannah Morning News

ROB ROGERS, Pittsburgh Post-Gazette

BOB ENGLEHART, Hartford Courant

DWANE POWELL, Raliegh News & Observer

MARK STREETER, Savannah Morning News

THOMAS BOLDT, Calgary Sun

OLLE JOHANSSON, Sweden

ED STEIN, Rocky Mountain News

"HAVE OUR EXPERTS AUTHENTICATE WHETHER IT'S AN AL QAIDA OR 700 CLUB TAPE."

HENRY PAYNE, Detroit News

Deep Throat

Washington Post reporter Bob Woodward refused to reveal the identity of his source for the Watergate scandal, but this year Deep Throat revealed himself to be Mark Felt, a former official at the FBI. Cartoonists reminisced about Richard Nixon and the scandals of the '70s.

ALEN
LAUZAN
FALCON
Chile

caglecartoons.com/espanol

MIKE LANE
Cagle Cartoons

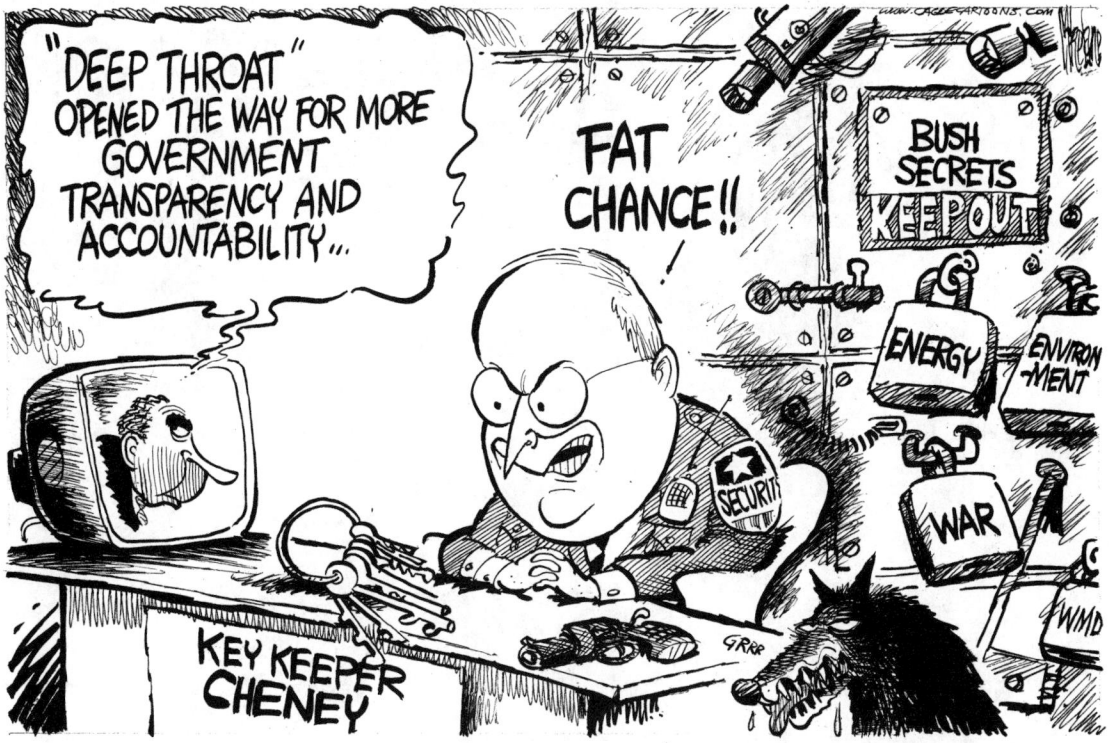

STAHLER.
©THE COLUMBUS DISPATCH.
2005.

DEEP THROAT

JEFF STAHLER
Columbus
Dispatch

BOB GORRELL, Creators Syndicate

ROBERT ARIAIL, The State (SC)

PATRICK O'CONNOR, Los Angeles Daily News

CLAY JONES, Freelance-Star (VA)

JACK OHMAN, Portland Oregonian

MARK STREETER, Savannah Morning News

DAN WASSERMAN, Boston Globe

CHRIS BRITT, State Journal-Register

STEVE BENSON, Arizona Republic

JOHN DEERING, Arkansas Democrat Gazette

BOB ENGLEHART, Hartford Courant

"That's right . . . Deep Throat was a traitor responsible for bringing down my presidency. I had nothing to do with it."

BRUCE BEATTIE, Daytona News-Journal

BILL DAY, Memphis Commercial Appeal

DEEP THROAT

STEVE SACK
Minneapolis Star-Tribune

JEFF PARKER, Florida Today

OLLE JOHANSSON, Sweden

TIM MENEES, Pittsburgh Post-Gazette

DEEP THROAT DISLODGES A CHICKEN BONE

KEN CATALINO, Creators Syndicate

ALAN LAUZAN FALCON, Chile

NATIONAL TREASURE

CAL GRONDAHL, Utah Standard Examiner

JOE HELLER, Green Bay Press-Gazette

SIGNE WILKINSON, Philadelphia Daily News

DEEP THROAT

CORKY TRINIDAD, Honolulu Star Bulletin

GARY MARKSTEIN, Copley News Service

JACK OHMAN, Portland Oregonian

STEVE BENSON, Arizona Republic

MIKE LESTER, Rome News-Tribune (GA)

ROBERT ARIAIL, The State (SC)

BRUCE PLANTE, Chattanooga Times Free Press

ED STEIN, Rocky Mountain News

PATRICK CHAPPATTE, International Herald Tribune

GARY VARVEL, Indianapolis Star

RICHARD CROWSON, Witchita Eagle

MATT DAVIES, Journal News (NY)

SCOTT STANTIS, Birmingham News

DICK WRIGHT, Columbus Dispatch

LLOYD DANGLE
Troubletown

R.J. MATSON, The New York Observer

JOE HELLER, Green Bay Press-Gazette

WALT HANDELSMAN, Newsday

DAN WASSERMAN, Boston Globe

DICK LOCHER, Chicago Tribune

CHIP BOK, Akron Beacon-Journal

MARSHALL RAMSEY, Clarion Ledger

MIKE THOMPSON, Detroit Free-Press

JEFF KOTERBA, Omaha World Herald

JONATHAN BROWN, Deseret News (UT)

MIKE LANE, Cagle Cartoons

MIKE KEEFE, Denver Post

Roberts and Miers

John Roberts didn't want to give specifics in the Senate hearings to confirm his nomination as chief justice of the United States. He refused to speak about issues that might face the Court, including abortion and the Roe v. Wade decision; he sought to appease Democrats by saying he was opposed to "judicial activism." A bigger "stealth nomination" came next, as President Bush nominated his personal lawyer, Harriet Miers, to a second vacancy on the high court. Miers had run the Texas Lottery under then-Governor Bush, and was a longtime Bush crony, with little record of her positions on the issues. Conservatives and liberals both found something to distrust about Miers.

DARYL CAGLE, Slate.com

JEN SORENSON, Slowpoke

BillDay The Commercial Appeal

BILL DAY, Memphis Commercial Appeal

JOHN TREVER, Albuquerque Journal

STAHLER.
©THE COLUMBUS DISPATCH. 2005.

JEFF STAHLER
Columbus Dispatch

DICK WRIGHT, Copley News Service

REX BABIN, Sacramento Bee

M.e. COHEN, National/Freelance

DAVID HORSEY, Seattle Post Intelligencer

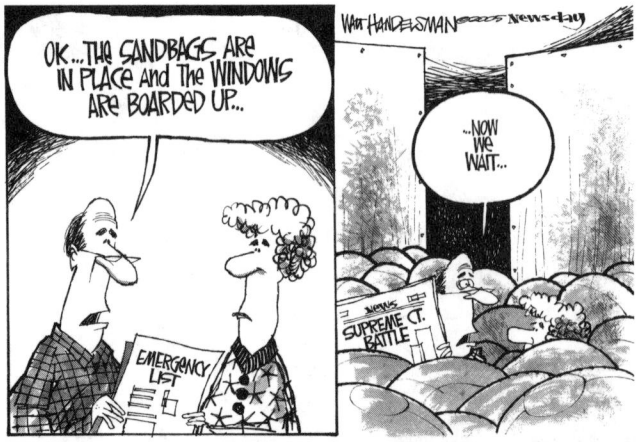

WALT HANDELSMAN, Newsday

VIC HARVILLE, Stephens Media Group

WALT HANDELSMAN, Newsday

MARK STREETER, Savannah Morning News

DARYL CAGLE, Slate.com

REX BABIN, Sacramento Bee

STEVE KELLEY, New Orleans Times Picayune

JOHN TREVER, Albuquerque Journal

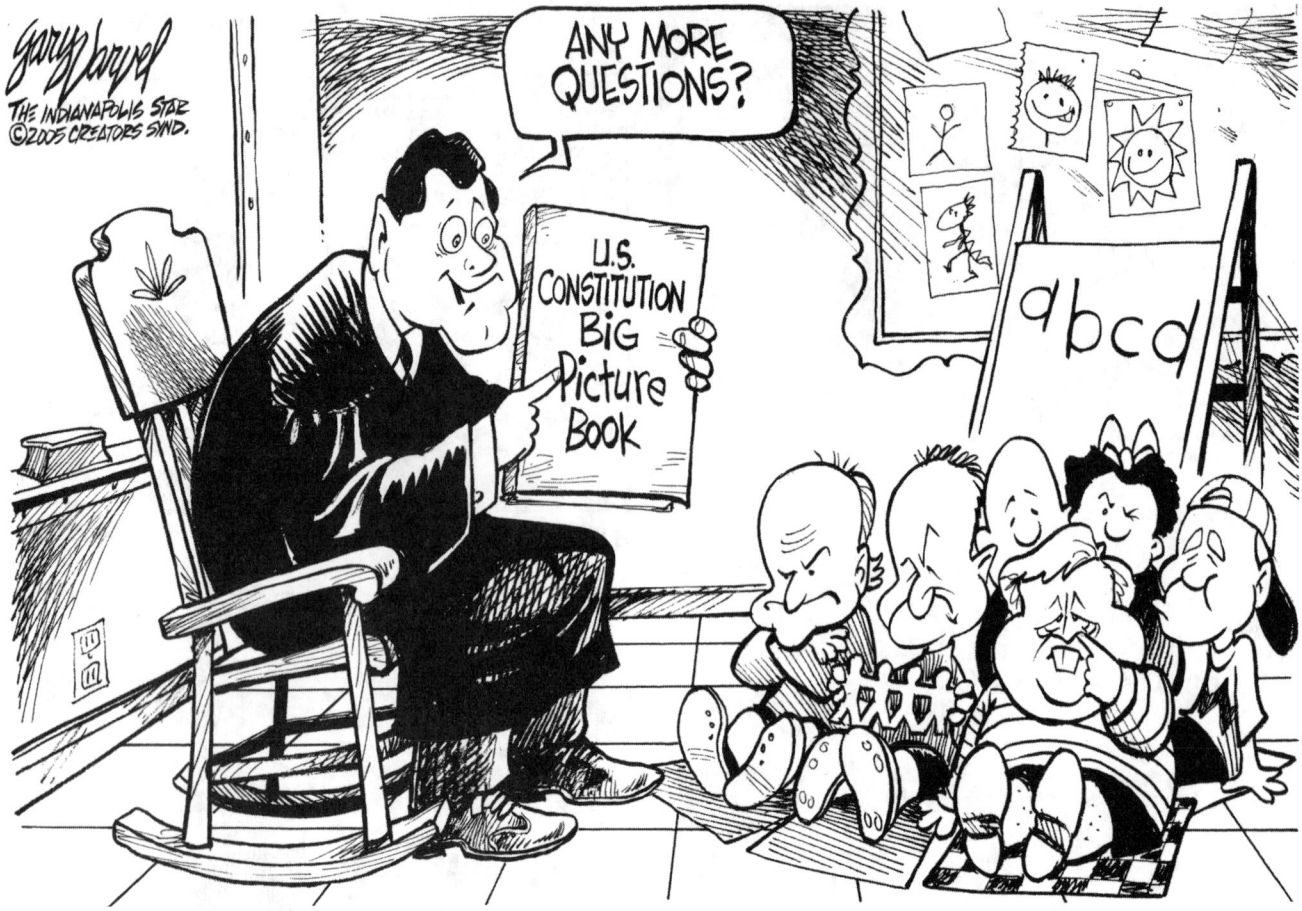

GARY VARVEL, Indianapolis Star

MIKE THOMPSON, Detroit Free Press

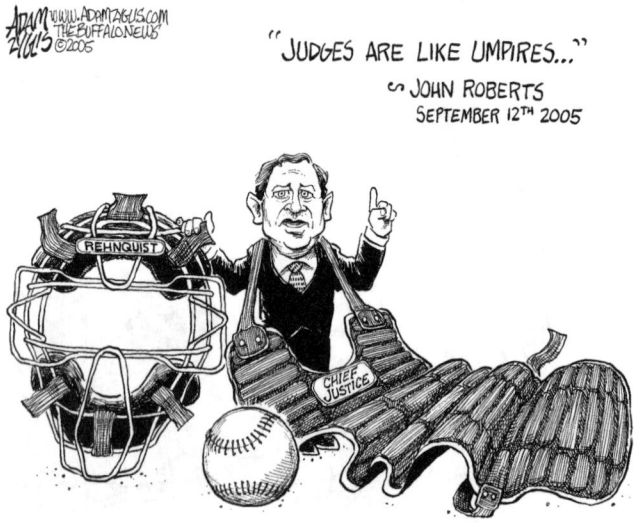

ADAM ZYGLIS, Buffalo News

ROBERTS & MIERS

ROBERT ARIAIL
The State (SC)

PATRICK O'CONNOR, Los Angeles Daily News

NATE BEELER, Washington Examiner

JOHN SHERFFIUS

NATE BEELER, Washington Examiner

MIKE THOMPSON, Detroit Free-Press

KEN CATALINO, National/Freelance

HENRY PAYNE, Detroit News

KIRK WALTERS
Toledo Blade

Democrats blocked Republican judicial nominees...Republicans retaliated by blocking Democratic judicial nominees... Democrats then retaliated for the retaliation by blocking Republican judicial nominees...

And on it went...

Until the entire Judicial Branch of the United States government consisted of Judge Edwin P. Partukey, 96, of the 6th District Court of Appeals.

ROBERT ARIAIL, The State (SC)

M.e. COHEN

JOHN BRANCH, San Antonio Express-News

MIKE LANE, Cagle Cartoons

DARYL CAGLE, MSNBC.com

JIM DAY, Las Vegas Review Journal

GARY BROOKINS, Richmond Times-Dispatch

KIRK WALTERS, Toledo Blade

MARSHALL RAMSEY, Clarion Ledger

SCOTT STANTIS, Birmingham News

MIKE LESTER, Rome News-Tribune (GA)

BOB ENGLEHART, Hartford Courant

JOHN DARKOW, Columbia Daily Tribune (MO)

ROBERT ARIAIL, The State (SC)

PAT BAGLEY, Salt Lake Tribune

Gas Prices

Gasoline prices topped $3 a gallon in 2005 as oil company profits skyrocketed. The price of crude oil reached new highs, but the high gasoline prices rose even higher. A lack of refining capacity, Hurricane Katrina, new demand from the growing economy in China, and oil company greed all combined to shock motorists.

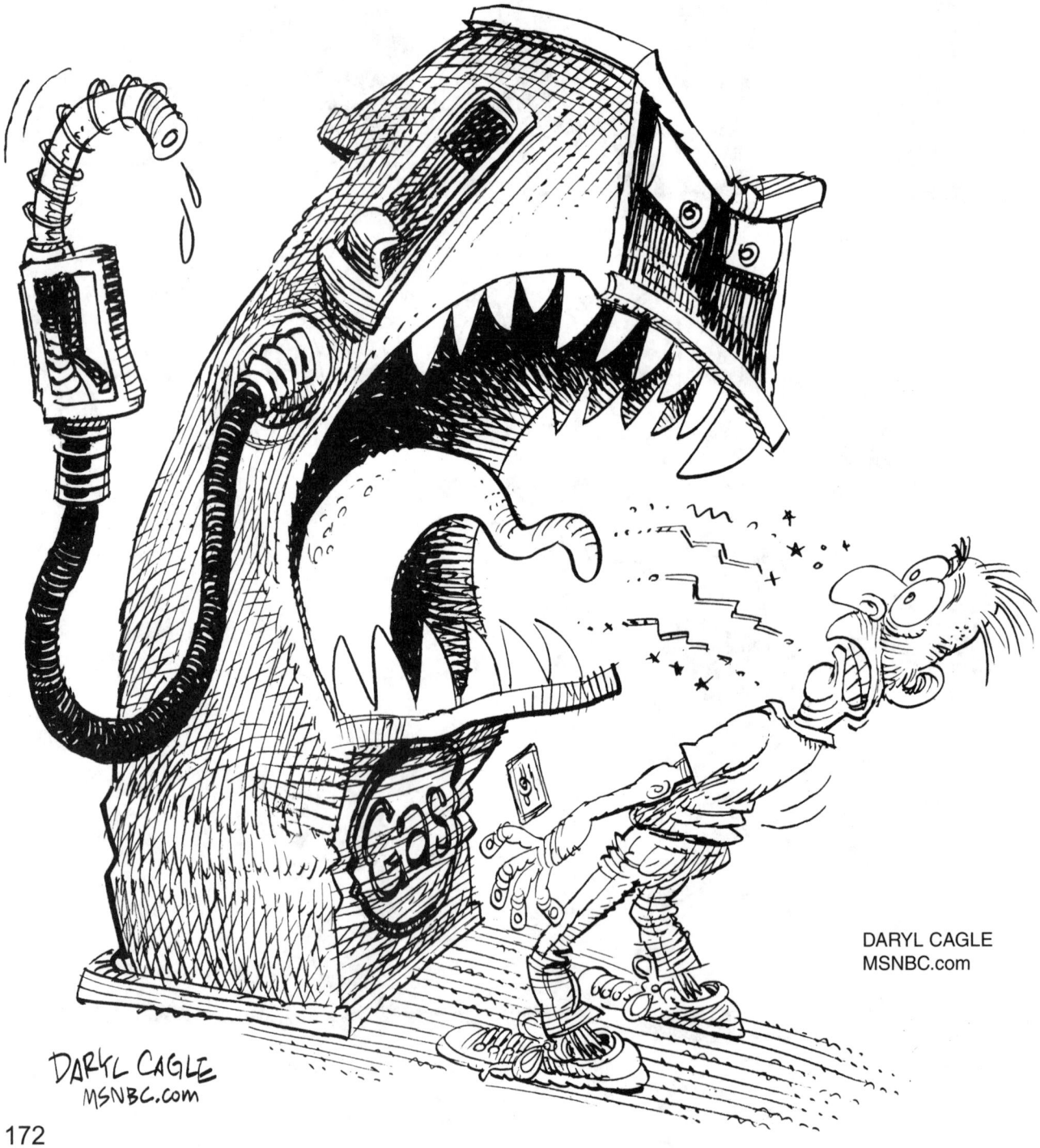

DARYL CAGLE
MSNBC.com

SLOWPOKE

JEN SORENSON, Slowpoke

©2005 Jen Sorensen

www.slowpokecomics.com

DOUG MARLETTE, Tallahassee Democrat

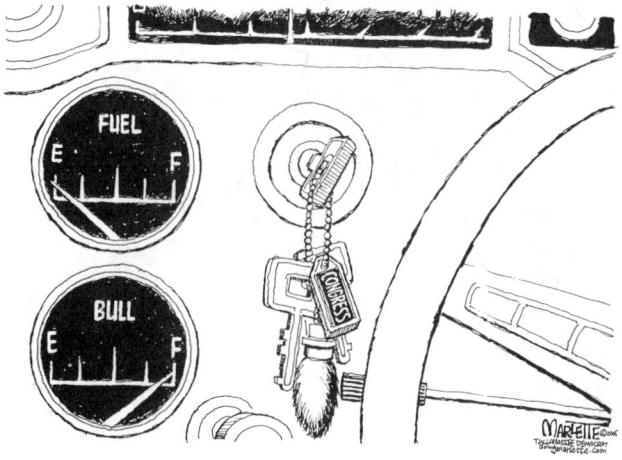

PAUL COMBS, Tampa Tribune

ZIPPCO

HEY, BUDDY... CAN YOU SPARE A CUP OF GAS?

STAYSKAL TRIBUNE MEDIA SERVICES 8/05

WAYNE STAYSKAL, Tribune Media Services

M.e. COHEN

NATE BEELER, Washington Examiner

WORLD'S LARGEST S.U.V. NOW ON SALE...

STEVE SACK
Minneapolis
Star-Tribune

—AND IT COMES WITH A HUMMER TO DRIVE YOURSELF UP TO THE PASSENGER COMPARTMENT!

SACK
STAR TRIBUNE

CAMERON CARDOW, Ottawa Citizen

JIMMY MARGULIES, The Record

STEVE NEASE, Oakville Beaver

M.e. COHEN

WALT HANDELSMAN, Newsday

SIGNE WILKINSON, Philadelphia Daily News

BOB ENGLEHART, Hartford Courant

DICK WRIGHT, Columbus Dispatch

DICK LOCHER, Chicago Tribune

STEVE BREEN, San Diego Union-Tribune

DANA SUMMERS, Orlando Sentinel

LARRY WRIGHT, Detroit News

PAUL CONRAD, Tribune Media Services

JOHN COLE, Scranton Times-Tribune

OLLE JOHANSSON, Sweden

NICK ANDERSON, Louisville Courier-Journal

"In memory of all those who have sacrificed their lives for oil, raise the price."

CAL GRONDAHL, Utah Standard Examiner

BRUCE PLANTE, Chattanooga Times Free Press

JOHN BRANCH, San Antonio Express-News

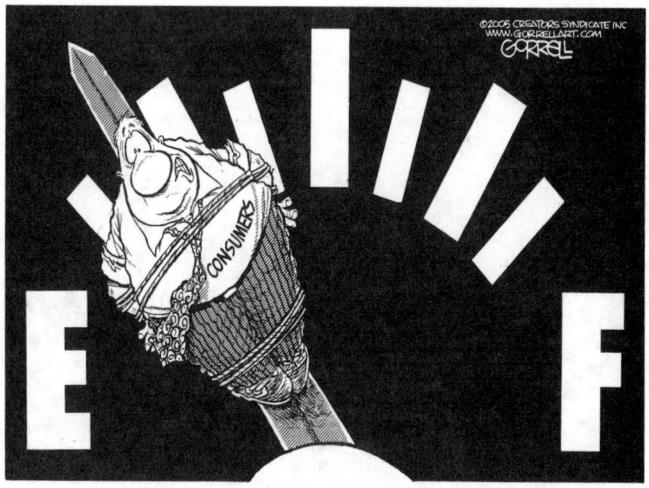

BOB GORRELL, Creators Syndicate

PAT BAGLEY, Salt Lake Tribune

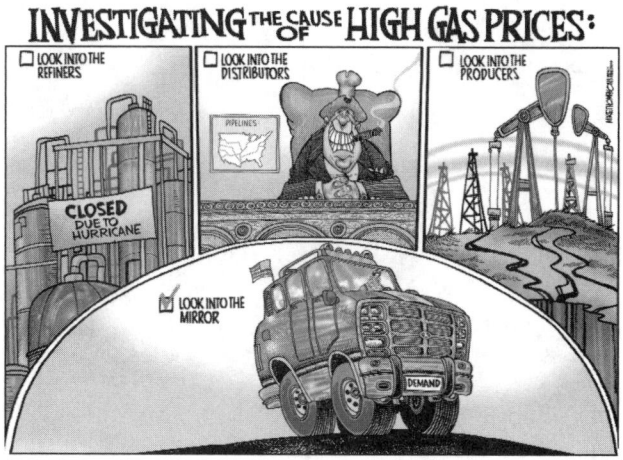

MIKE THOMPSON, Detroit Free-Press

BRIAN FAIRRINGTON, Cagle Cartoons

STEVE SACK, Minneapolis Star-Tribune

VIC HARVILLE, Stephens Media Group

JOHN DEERING, Arkansas Democrat Gazette

PETAR PISMESTROVIC, Austria

PATRICK CHAPPATTE, International Herald Tribune

PATRICK O'CONNOR, Los Angeles Daily News

ROBERT ARIAIL, The State (SC)

JOE HELLER, Green Bay Press-Gazette

Memorable Moments of Summer Vacation 2005

BRUCE BEATTIE, Daytona News-Journal

VINCE O'FARRELL, Australia

BRIAN FAIRRINGTON, Cagle Cartoons

DARYL CAGLE
Slate.com

CHIP BOK, Akron Beacon-Journal

TIM MENEES, Pittsburgh Post-Gazette

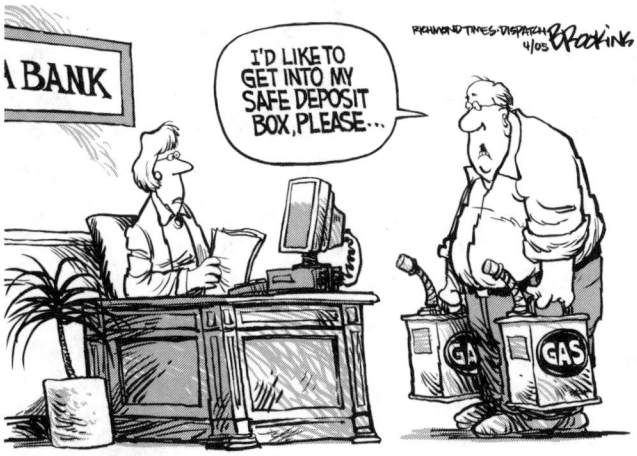

GARY BROOKINS, Richmond Times-Dispatch

VIC HARVILLE, Stephens Media Group

"WELCOME TO MY EXTREME ANGER MANAGEMENT SEMINAR."

KEN CATALINO, Creators Syndicate

VINCE O'FARRELL, Cagle Cartoons

STEVE KELLEY, New Orleans Times Picayune

CAMERON CARDOW, Ottawa Citizen

Newsweek

Newsweek reported that during interrogations of suspected terrorists, military officials had flushed the Quran down the toilet. The story sparked deadly protests around the world, but was soon found to be false—a tip on "deep background" gone horribly wrong. Cartoonists had a field day as yet another bastion of journalism went down the toilet. Cartoonists love to draw toilets.

STEVE BREEN, San Diego Union-Tribune

JONATHAN BROWN, Deseret News

JOHN SHERFFIUS

BRUCE PLANTE, Chattanooga Times Free Press

JEFF KOTERBA, Omaha World Herald

J.D. CROWE, Mobile Register

JOE HELLER, Green Bay Press-Gazette

ERIC ALLIE, Pioneer Press (IL)

ROBERT ARIAIL, The State (SC)

RICHARD CROWSON, Witchita Eagle

PAT BAGLEY, Salt Lake Tribune

DOUG MARLETTE, Tallahassee Democrat

STEVE BENSON, Arizona Republic

"LOOK...SEE?...I'M FLUSHING A NEWSWEEK DOWN THE TOILET..."

CORKY TRINIDAD, Honolulu Star Bulletin

CAMERON CARDOW, Ottawa Citizen

OLLE JOHANSSON, Sweden

BOB GORRELL, Creators Syndicate

STEPHANE PERAY, Thailand

BOB ENGLEHART, Hartford Courant

ED STEIN, Rocky Mountain News

TIM MENEES, Pittsburgh Post-Gazette

CHRIS BRITT, State Journal-Register

DAN WASSERMAN, Boston Globe

SCOTT STANTIS, Birmingham News

PAUL COMBS, Tampa Tribune

MIKE LANE, Cagle Cartoons

CHRISTO KOMARNITSKI, Bulgaria

SANDY HUFFAKER, Cagle Cartoons

HENRY PAYNE, Detroit News

DICK LOCHER, Chicago Tribune

DWAYNE BOOTH, Mr. Fish

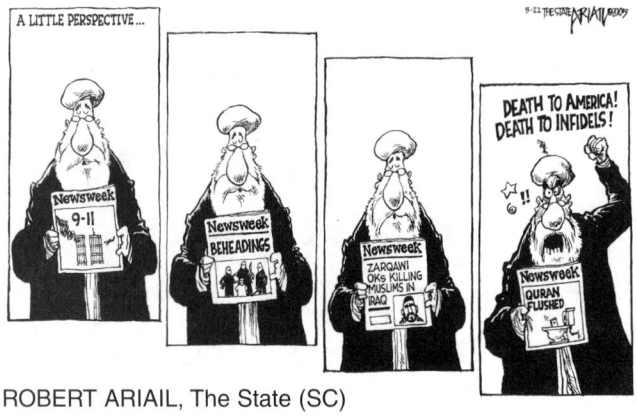

ROBERT ARIAIL, The State (SC)

DAVID HORSEY, Seattle Post Intelligencer

CHIP BOK, Akron Beacon-Journal

ROB ROGERS, Pittsburgh Post-Gazette

VIC HARVILLE, Stephens Media Group

MIKE LESTER, Rome News-Tribune (GA)

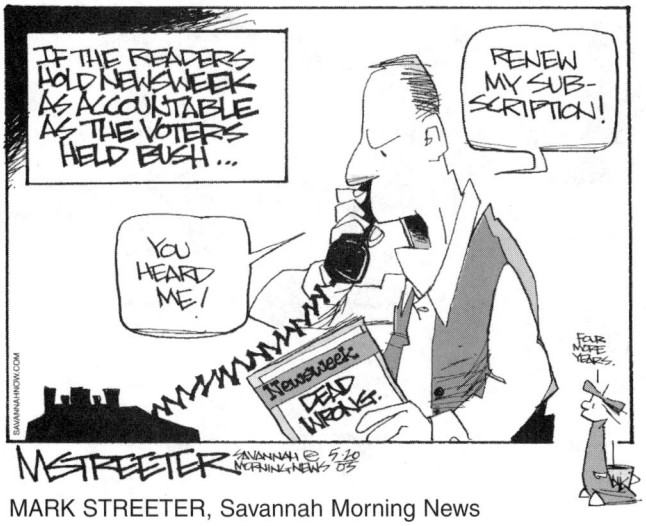

MARK STREETER, Savannah Morning News

DWANE POWELL, Raleigh News & Observer

NICK ANDERSON, Louisville Courier-Journal

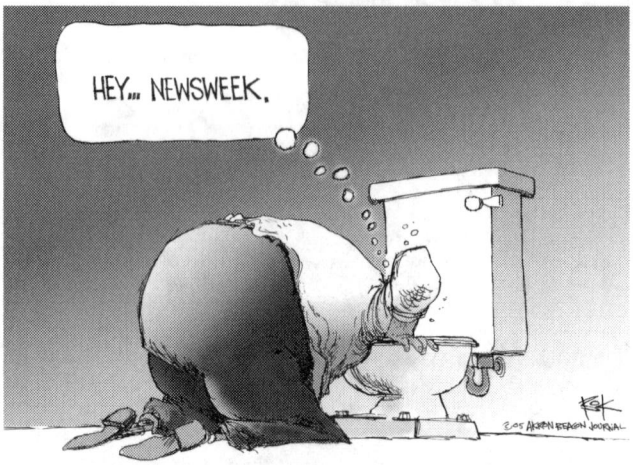

WORSHIPPING AT THE PORCELAIN SHRINE

CHIP BOK, Akron Beacon-Journal

CLAY BENNETT, Christian Science Monitor

JOHN COLE, Scranton Times-Tribune

MIKE KEEFE, Denver Post

THOMAS BOLDT, Calgary Sun

GOOD NEWS. WE'VE RETRACTED THE STORY...

AFGHAN RIOT VICTIMS

MIKE RAMIREZ, Los Angeles Times

THOMAS BOLDT
Calgary Sun

PATRICK O'CONNOR, Los Angeles Daily News

ARE THEY COMPARING ME TO DARTH VADER?

LET'S RIOT OVER THAT NEXT.

Newsweek

2005 STAHLER.
©THE COLUMBUS DISPATCH

JEFF STAHLER, Columbus Dispatch

BILL SCHORR

LARRY WRIGHT, Detroit News

STEVE KELLEY, New Orleans Times Picayune

REX BABIN, Sacramento Bee

ADAM ZYGLIS, Buffalo News

Iraq

Suicide bombers continued to kill American soldiers and Iraqi civilians in a low-grade civil war between Sunnis and Shiites. There was an election where Iraqis braved the violence to vote in large numbers. A new constitution for Iraq was proposed and debated. President Bush and his "neo-con" supporters forged ahead, racking up debt, death tolls, and many less-than-flattering editorial cartoons.

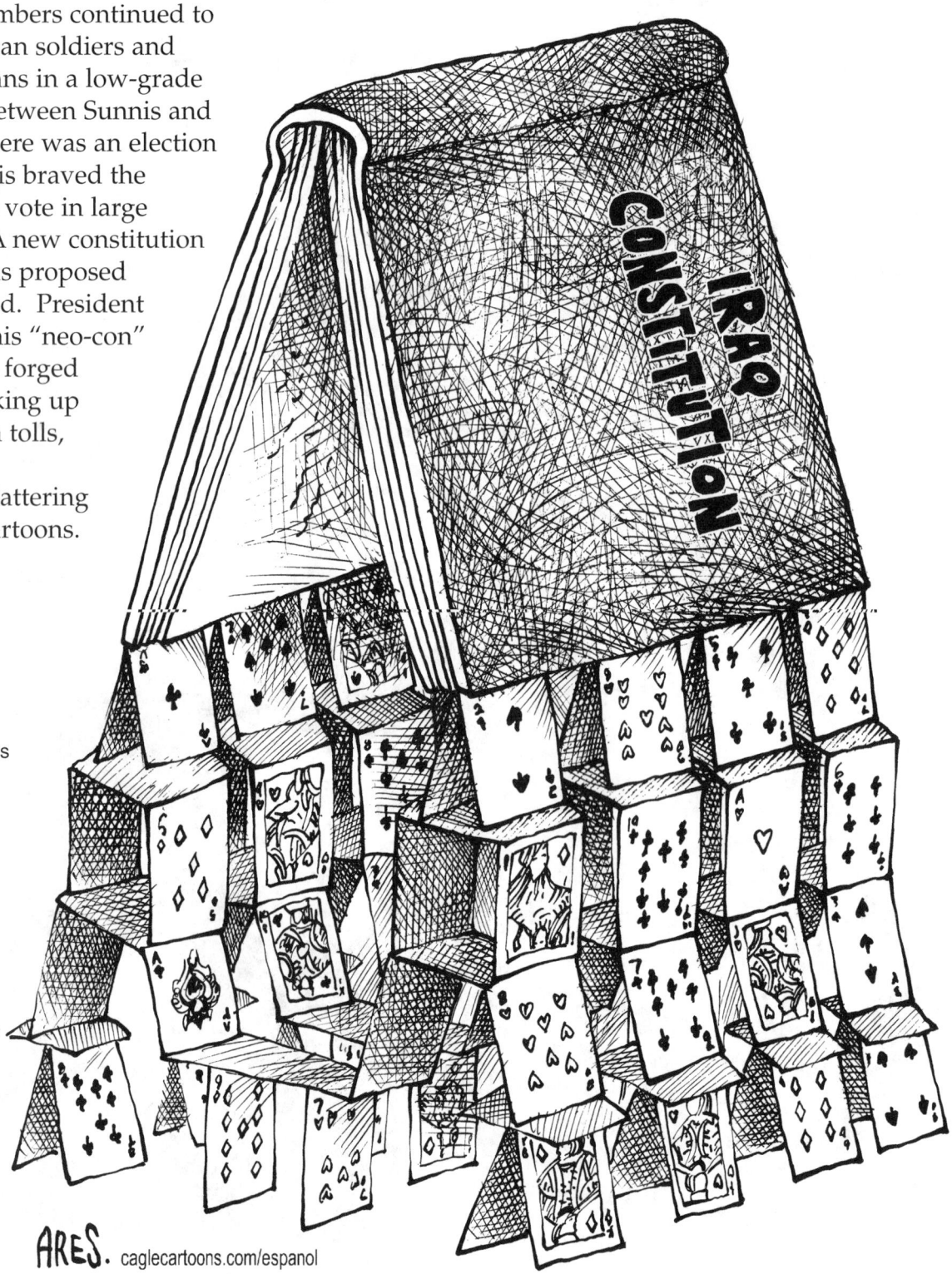

ARES
Cagle Cartoons

ALEN LAUZAN FALCON, Chile

MIKE LESTER, Rome News-Tribune (GA)

JAMES CASCIARI Scripps Howard News Service

caglecartoons.com/espa

ARES
Cagle Cartoons
caglecartoons.com/espanol

MIKE KEEFE, Denver Post

GUY BADO, Journal Le Droit (Ottawa)

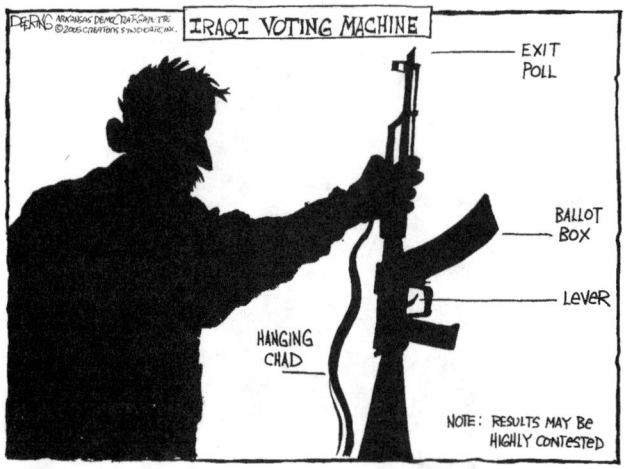

JOHN DEERING, Arkansas Democrat Gazette

STEVE NEASE, Oakville Beaver

CHIP BOK, Akron Beacon-Journal

PATRICK CHAPPATTE, International Herald Tribune

DANA SUMMERS, Orlando Sentinel

PATRICK O'CONNOR, Los Angeles Daily News

ROBERT ARIAIL, The State (SC)

DREW SHENEMAN, Newark Star-Ledger

ANGEL BOLIGAN
Mexico

BILL SCHORR, AM New York

RECONSTRUCTION IS MY PRIORITY.

deadder.net

MICHAEL DeADDER, Daily News, Halifax, Nova Scotia

CHUCK ASAY, Colorado Springs Gazette

KIRK ANDERSON

DEMOCRACY IN THE BUSH MOLD

ANDY SINGER
No Exit

DREW SHENEMAN
Newark Star-Ledger

STEVE SACK, Minneapolis Star-Tribune

FEEDBACK

GRAEME MACKAY, Hamilton Spectator

ETTA HULME
Ft. Worth Star Telegram

WRITER'S BLOCK

ED STEIN
Rocky Mountain News

"He can help us write an Iraqi constitution that's acceptable to all . . .
He's one of the best divorce attorneys in the business."

BRUCE BEATTIE, Daytona News-Journal

JACK OHMAN, Portland Oregonian

"We didn't get much of anything in Iraq's new constitution. We hear you have some new vacancies in the neighborhood."

BRUCE BEATTIE, Daytona News-Journal

MARIE WOOLF, Cagle Cartoons

JIMMY MARGULIES, The Record (NJ)

STEVE SACK, Minneapolis Star-Tribune

IRAQ

IRAQI *constitutional* BUTCHER CHART

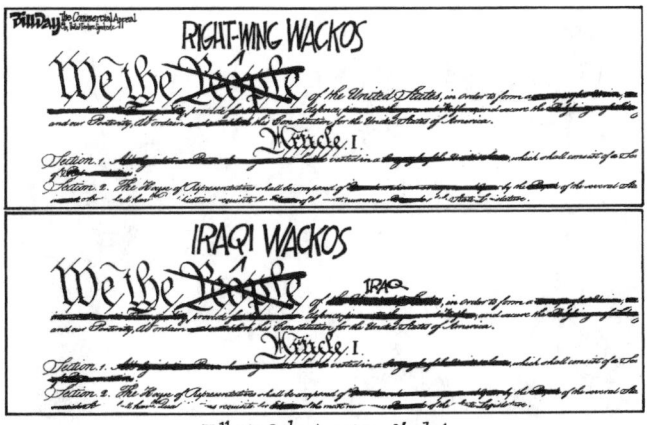

BILL DAY, Memphis Commercial Appeal

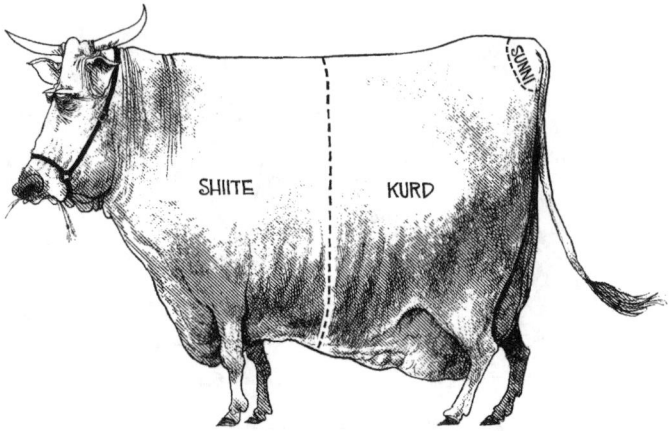

MIKE RAMIREZ, Los Angeles Times

JOHN DARKOW, Columbia Daily Tribune (MO)

DANA SUMMERS, Orlando Sentinel

DOUG MARLETTE, Tallahassee Democrat

STEPHANE PERAY, The Nation, Thailand

VINCE O'FARRELL, Australia

CHIP BOK, Akron Beacon-Journal

HENRY PAYNE, Detroit News

JEFF KOTERBA, Omaha World Herald

RANDY BISH, Pittsburgh Tribune-Review

Cindy Sheehan

Cindy Sheehan camped out at the gates of President Bush's Texas ranch, saying she wouldn't leave until she spoke with the president about her Marine son Casey's death in Iraq. Sheehan had spoken to Bush in June of 2004, but hadn't expressed her grievances about the war. Bush refused to meet with Sheehan this time, and the story snowballed in a blizzard of press coverage. Sheehan soon left the president's ranch to begin a national tour protesting the war. Supporters of the president quoted some of Sheehan's less eloquent statements and painted her as a radical because she was supported by the likes of Michael Moore.

DARYL CAGLE, MSNBC.com

JEFF KOTERBA, Omaha World Herald

LARRY WRIGHT, Detroit News

LLOYD DANGLE, Troubletown

JEFF PARKER, Florida Today

"WHY IS THAT DEAD SOLDIER'S MOM PICKING ON ME?"

R.J. MATSON, St. Louis Post Dispatch

DAN WASSERMAN, Boston Globe

MIKE KEEFE
Denver Post

REX BABIN
Sacramento Bee

SMEAR CAMPAIGN

WALT HANDELSMAN, Newsday

JEFF STAHLER, Columbus Dispatch

Crawford Chicken Ranch

JOHN SHERFFIUS

CHRIS BRITT, State Journal-Register

DOUG MARLETTE, Tallahassee Democrat

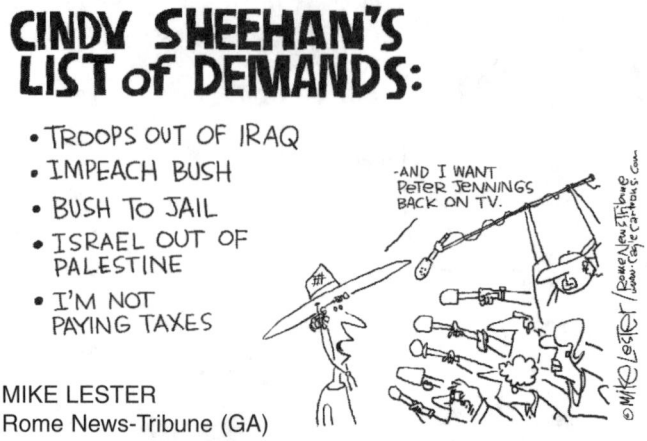

MIKE LESTER
Rome News-Tribune (GA)

DARYL CAGLE, MSNBC.com

CHRISTO KOMARNITSKI
Bulgaria

VIC HARVILLE, Stephens Media Group

ROBERT ARIAIL, The State (SC)

MARK STREETER, Savannah Morning News

TAYLOR JONES
Tribune Media Services

OH, GIVE ME A HOME WHERE THE BUFFALO ROAM
WHERE THE DEER AND THE ANTELOPE PLAY;
WHERE NEVER IS HEARD A DISCOURAGIN' WORD,
AND THE SKY IS NOT CLOUDED ALL DAY.

OUT OF IRAQ

WHY DID MY SON HAVE TO DIE?

Ottawa Citiz
Caglecartoons.

CAMERON CARDOW, Ottawa Citizen

PATRICK O'CONNOR, Los Angeles Daily News

THOMAS BOLDT, Calgary Sun

CHRISTO KOMARNITSKI, Bulgaria

CLAY JONES, Freelance-Star (VA)

CHUCK ASAY, Colorado Springs Gazette

Hear No Grieving Mother

See No Grieving Mother

Speak to No Grieving Mother

STEVE BENSON
Arizona Republic

DREW SHENEMAN
Newark Star-Ledger

FINALLY WORKING ON AN EXIT STRATEGY

STEVE SACK, Minneapolis Star-Tribune

VINCE O'FARRELL, Australia

PAT BAGLEY, Salt Lake Tribune

REX BABIN, Sacramento Bee

"MRS. SHEEHAN STOP I FEEL YOUR GRIEF STOP SIGNED..."

CORKY TRINIDAD, Honolulu Star Bulletin

MIKE LESTER, Rome News-Tribune (GA)

Hurricane Katrina

Hurricane Katrina devastated the Gulf Coast. The storm surge breached levees in New Orleans, flooding the city and killing more than 1,000 people in the region. The tragedy was made worse by the government's slow response. Officials claimed that they couldn't reach areas that reporters reached easily—and America watched on television—as victims cried out for help from their rooftops. White House officials and apologists tried to marginalize critics by calling the situation "the blame game" and saying that it was not the time for "pointing fingers." The president's approval ratings dropped to their lowest ever. Federal Emergency Management Agency Director Michael Brown resigned amid scathing criticism and the revelation that he had padded his résumé; his last job was organizing horse shows. The swirling morass of controversy and tragedy inspired cartoons from around the world.

JACK OHMAN, Portland Oregonian

DICK WRIGHT, Copley News Service

THOMAS BOLDT, Calgary Sun

ADAM ZYGLIS, Buffalo News

BOB ENGLEHART, Hartford Courant

PETAR PISMESTROVIC, Austria

MIKE LESTER, Rome News-Tribune (GA)

ERIC ALLIE, Pioneer Press (IL)

KIRK WALTERS
Toledo Blade

CHRIS BRITT, State Journal-Register

MATT DAVIES, Journal News (NY)

RIBER HANSSON, Sweden

DANA SUMMERS, Orlando Sentinel

LALO ALCARAZ, L.A. Weekly

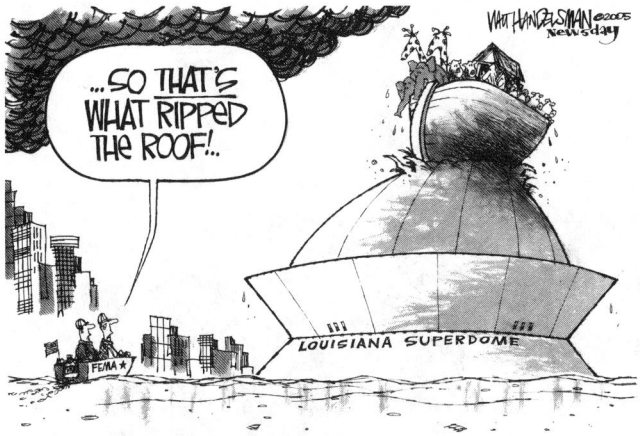

WALT HANDELSMAN, Newsday

TIM MENEES, Pittsburgh Post-Gazette

KIRK WALTERS, Toledo Blade

CORKY TRINIDAD, Honolulu Star Bulletin

BILOXI
GULF PORT
MOBILE

STEVE KELLEY
New Orleans
Times Picayune

STEPHANE PERAY
Thailand

SCOTT STANTIS, Birmingham News

STEVE SACK, Minneapolis Star-Tribune

STEVE BENSON, Arizona Republic

SANDY HUFFAKER, Cagle Cartoons

REX BABIN, Sacramento Bee

NATE BEELER
Washington Examiner

DARYL CAGLE MSNBC.com DARYL CAGLE, MSNBC.com

JOHN BRANCH, San Antonio Express-News

DAN WASSERMAN, Boston Globe

MILT PRIGGEE

PAT BAGLEY
Salt Lake Tribune

SERGIO LANGER
Argentina

OSMANI SIMANCA, Brazil

JOHN COLE, Scranton Times Tribune

Peter Jennings

World-renowned television news anchor Peter Jennings passed away at 67 from lung cancer. Jennings had given up smoking, only to start again on 9/11. In one of his last public statements, he expressed his regrets, urging everyone not to smoke. Cartoonists paid tribute to a consummate newsman and repeated his warnings to smokers in their memorial cartoons.

JOHN COLE
Scranton Times-Tribune

MIKE RAMIREZ
Los Angeles Times

KIRK ©2005 The Toledo Blade email: kirk@theblade.com

KIRK WALTERS
Toledo Blade

DARYL CAGLE, MSNBC.com

THOMAS BOLDT, Calgary Sun

JOE HELLER, Green Bay Press-Gazette

MARK STREETER, Savannah Morning News

CORKY TRINIDAD, Honolulu Star Bulletin

VIC HARVILLE, Stephens Media Group

In Memoriam

Memorial cartoons are always the most popular cartoons. Pope John Paul II, Peter Jennings, and Terri Schiavo are memorialized in other chapters of this book. Other noteworthy people who passed away this year included Rosa Parks, Chief Justice William Rehnquist, Eddie Albert, Bob Denver, Johnny Carson, Johnnie Cochran, Reggie White, Will Eisner, and Nazi hunter Simon Wiesenthal.

BILL DAY, Memphis Commercial Appeal

BOB ENGLEHART, Hartford Courant

MIKE KEEFE, Denver Post

JACK OHMAN, Portland Oregonian

"FIRST TIME I'VE EVER BEEN IN THE GUEST SEAT..."

CORKY TRINIDAD, Honolulu Star Bulletin

JOHNNY CARSON- 1925-2005

RANDY BISH, Pittsburgh Tribune-Review

"SOMEONE WILL BE TAKING A LONG, LONG TRIP."

PAUL CONRAD, Tribune Media Services

DARYL CAGLE, Slate.com

ROBERT ARIAIL, The State (SC)

JOHNNY CARSON • 1925 - 2005

STEVE NEASE, Oakville Beaver

JOHN BRANCH, San Antonio Express-News

MARK STREETER, Savannah Morning News

MICHAEL RAMIREZ, Los Angeles Times

STEVE BREEN, San Diego Union-Tribune

KEN CATALINO, Creators Syndicate

CORKY TRINIDAD, Honolulu Star Bulletin

O.J. CALLED... TURNS OUT THE GLOVE *DID* FIT

RANDY BISH, Pittsburgh Tribune-Review

HENRY PAYNE, Detroit News

MARSHALL RAMSEY, Clarion Ledger

DARYL CAGLE
MSNBC.com

BOB ENGLEHART, Hartford Courant

MARK STREETER, Savannah Morning News

JOE HELLER, Green Bay Press-Gazette

SANDY HUFFAKER
Cagle Cartoons

MIKE KEEFE
Denver Post

R.J. MATSON, St. Louis Post Dispatch

caglecartoons.com

VISITORS PASS

N-Z

© MATSON ST.LOUIS POST-DISPATCH

"REST ASSURED, MR. WIESENTHAL, THEY'RE ALL PRESENT AND ACCOUNTED FOR..."

OLLE JOHANSSON, Sweden

STEVE GREENBERG, Ventura County Star

www.reuben.org/lailson

Will Eisner 1917 2005

Lailson 050105

LAILSON DE HOLLANDA, Brazil

MARK STREETER, Savannah Morning News

JONATHAN BROWN, Deseret News

Pulitzer Prize

The Pulitzer Prize is the most prestigious award in the editorial cartooning profession. Cartoonists submit a portfolio of 20 cartoons for review by two committees at Columbia University. The 2005 winner was Nick Anderson of the Louisville Courier-Journal, for this selection of cartoons that was published in 2004.

Nick does two versions of each of his cartoons: the black line art version that we show here, and a charming watercolor version. His portfolio was unusual in that all of his cartoons were colorful paintings.

HEALTH·CO DRUG DISCOUNT CARD
HMO·CO Drug Discount Card
BIG MEDS DRUG DISCOUNT CARD
DRUG DISCOUNT CARD
Med·Conglom Drug DISCOUNT Card
ACME DRUG DISCOUNT CARD
DISCOUNT CARD
DRUG DISCOUNT CARD
MED-Rx Discount CARD
Drug·Co DISCOUNT Card
BEST MEDS DRUG DISCOUNT CARD
ACME DRUG DISCOUNT CARD
NICK ANDERSON 5.13 BY COURIER-JOURNAL WWW.NICKANDERSONCARTOONS.COM

SADDAM HUSSEIN WANTS TO HIRE YOUR LAWYERS...
TORTURE JUSTIFIED (IF COMMANDER-IN-CHIEF DEEMS IT NECESSARY)
-JUSTICE DEPT.

IRAQ
PARDON OUR PROGRESS!!
NICK ANDERSON 6.11.04
COURIER-JOURNAL
WWW.NICKANDERSONCARTOONS.COM

HOW'S OUR DRIVING?
CALL
1·800·F#@*·OFF
CIVILITY
GENEVA CONVENTIO
We the People
ENVIRONMENT
FISCAL RESPONSIBILITY
NICKANDERSON © 6·30·04 · COURIER-JOURNAL
www.NICKANDERSONCARTOONS.com

NICKANDERSON
©11·14·04 COURIER-JOURNAL
www.NICKANDERSONCARTOONS.COM

What's Wrong with This Picture?

GRILLED HOT DOGS

USA

USA

USA

USA

NICK ANDERSON © 8-17-04 COURIER-JOURNAL
WWW.NICKANDERSONCARTOONS.COM

NICK ANDERSON © 8-24-04 COURIER-JOURNAL
WWW.NICKANDERSONCARTOONS.COM

RUTH!

MISSION ACCOMPLISHED

SWIFT BOAT THUGS FOR BUSH

"IF YOU DON'T SALUTE, YOU'RE NOT A PATRIOT...."

I'D FEEL A LOT BETTER IF THE GUY IN FRONT WOULD STOP YELLING "WHEEEEEEE!"
PHARMACEUTICAL COMPANIES
HEALTH CARE COSTS

HE'S BROUGHT US THIS FAR.... LET'S SEE HOW FAR HE CAN TAKE US...
POLITICS OF FEAR

OH, SORRY KID....
P&P
STEROIDS

GAYS

THE other AXIS of EVIL...
MURDEROUS REGIMES
HUNGER
AIDS
AFRICA

IRAQI SECURITY FORCES

AT LAST, A PERFECT EMPLOYEE....
BLIND LOYALTY
NICKANDERSON ©12-16-04 COURIER-JOURNAL
WWW.NICKANDERSONCARTOONS.COM
APOLOGIES TO ROBERT MINOR

ANIMAL FARM
REVOLUTION!
STOP THE ABUSE OF POWER
DELAY
RESTORE HONOR AND INTEGRITY
HOUSE G.O.P.
NICKANDERSON ©11-19-04 COURIER-JOURNAL
WWW.NICKANDERSONCARTOONS.COM

Artists Index

A

Adcock, Brian, 63, 134, 135, 136
Alcaraz, Lalo, 59, 223
Allie, Eric, 18, 72, 100, 186, 221
Anderson, Kirk, 13, 200
Anderson, Nick, 63, 178, 192, 242, 243, 244, 245, 246, 247, 248, 249
Ares, 49, 196, 197
Ariail, Robert, 15, 75, 150, 156, 169, 171, 186, 190, 199, 213, 236
Asay, Chuck, 52, 75, 92, 114, 200, 215

B

Babin, Rex, 107, 111, 115, 121, 164, 165, 195, 211, 217, 226
Bado, Guy, 198
Bagley, Pat, 40, 68, 84, 143, 171, 179, 186, 217, 228
Beattie, Bruce, 5, 22, 74, 152, 203, 204
Beeler, Nate, 23, 25, 46, 51, 65, 69, 84, 113, 117, 167, 168, 174, 226
Bennet, Clay, 77, 93, 128, 192
Benson, Steve, 62, 79, 105, 128, 145, 151, 156, 187, 216, 226
Bish, Randy, 28, 137, 207, 235, 237
Bok, Chip, 6, 52, 72, 105, 113, 142, 160, 191, 192, 198, 207
Boldt, Thomas, 2, 65, 81, 87, 99, 127, 137, 147, 176, 192, 193, 214, 219, 232
Boligan, Angel, 124, 126, 199
Booth, Dwayne, 104, 106, 190
Branch, John, 111, 125, 169, 179, 227, 236
Breen, Steve, 27, 46, 60, 75, 123, 128, 141, 177, 185, 237
Britt, Chris, 4, 29, 40, 60, 145, 151, 188, 212, 222
Brookins, Gary, 24, 42, 52, 62, 131, 170
Brown, Jonathan, 92, 161, 185, 241

C

Cagle, Daryl, x, xi, 44, 50, 51, 63, 64, 73, 82, 85, 91, 93, 95, 102, 112, 116, 129, 144, 162, 165, 169, 172, 208, 212, 227, 232, 236, 238
Cardow, Cameron, 6, 34, 35, 52, 96, 105, 135, 142, 175, 187, 214
Casciari, James, 197
Catalino, Ken, 74, 84, 118, 154, 168, 237
Catrow, David, 48
Chappatte, Patrick, 16, 33, 59, 88, 157, 180, 198
Cohen, M.e., 12, 45, 77, 113, 164, 169, 174, 176
Cole, John, 34, 65, 178, 192, 229, 230
Combs, Paul, 4, 53, 96, 101, 127, 173, 189
Conrad, Paul, 57, 67, 72, 177, 235
Crowe, J.D., 15, 17, 52, 59, 106, 118, 185
Crowson, Richard, 144, 157, 186

D

Dangle, Lloyd, 159, 209
Darkow, John, 38, 171, 206
Davies, Matt, 3, 11, 14, 22, 78, 88, 92, 113, 119, 158, 222
Day, Bill, 50, 152, 163, 205, 234

Day, Jim, 85, 114, 169
de Hollanda, Lailson, 86, 241
Deadder, Michael, 146, 200
Deering, John, 6, 22, 24, 31, 54, 151, 180, 198
Devericks, Eric, 116

E - F - G

Englehart, Bob, 15, 37, 118, 124, 146, 152, 170, 176, 188, 220, 235, 238
Esquivel, Arcadio, 76, 88

Fairrington, Brian, vi, x, xi, 21, 26, 50, 57, 96, 120, 180
Falcon, Alen Lauzan, 133, 148, 154, 197
Fitzsimmons, David, 62, 78

Gorrell, Bob, 11, 25, 41, 46, 53, 74, 139, 150, 179, 187
Graston, Mike, 29, 107
Greenberg, Steve, 8, 25, 65, 71, 101, 240
Grondahl, Cal, 61, 154, 179

H

Hallaj, Emad, 134
Handelsman, Walt, 60, 130, 160, 164, 165, 176, 211, 223
Hansson, Riber, 18, 222
Harville, Vic, 48, 100, 144, 180, 191, 212, 233
Heller, Joe, 23, 38, 47, 62, 75, 101, 105, 141, 154, 160, 186, 232, 239
Horsey, David, 21, 59, 74, 86, 115, 141, 164, 190
Huffaker, Sandy, 18, 23, 28, 34, 96, 144, 189, 226, 239
Hulme, Etta, 116, 202

I - J - K

Johansson, Olle, 11, 147, 153, 178, 187, 240
Jones, Clay, 29, 41, 53, 142, 150, 215
Jones, Taylor, 110, 138, 213

Keefe, Mike, 6, 14, 18, 29, 48, 71, 87, 123, 125, 161, 192, 198, 211, 235, 239
Kelley, Steve, 36, 43, 47, 55, 59, 81, 141, 165, 195, 225
Komarnitski, Christo, 15, 33, 135, 142, 189, 212, 215
Koterba, Jeff, 11, 104, 132, 161, 185, 207, 209

L - M - N

Lane, Mike, 11, 42, 71, 94, 118, 149, 161, 169, 189
Langer, Sergio, 86, 229
Lester, Mike, 7, 35, 41, 47, 53, 54, 55, 56, 91, 94, 95, 108,
131, 143, 156, 170, 191, 197, 212, 217, 220
Lewis, Peter, 132
Locher, Dick, 42, 45, 48, 80, 87, 122, 160, 177, 189

Mackay, Graeme, 83, 109, 202
Margulies, Jimmy, 4, 29, 78, 99, 119, 175, 204
Markstein, Gary, 25, 122, 142, 155
Marlette, Doug, 17, 27, 57, 77, 105, 173, 186, 206, 212
Matson, R.J., 39, 45, 67, 91, 160, 210, 240
Menees, Tim, 77, 96, 130, 154, 188, 223
Mikula, Mike, 75

Nease, Steve, 3, 49, 60, 86, 108, 128, 176, 198, 236
Neril Licon, Antonio, 19, 77, 86, 122, 253

O - P

O'Connor, Patrick, 24, 25, 30, 42, 46, 74, 150, 167, 193, 199, 214
O'Farrell, Vince, 10, 33, 34, 62, 78, 96, 207, 217
Ohman, Jack, 8, 40, 53, 142, 150, 156, 203, 218, 235

Parker, Jeff, 68, 70, 79, 89, 107, 108, 128, 139, 153, 210
Payne, Henry, 80, 82, 89, 107, 146, 147, 168, 189, 207, 237
Peray, Stephane, 34, 74, 78, 136, 137, 187, 207, 225
Pismestrovic, Petar, 127, 180, 220
Plante, Bruce, 43, 47, 72, 101, 104, 156, 179, 185
Powell, Dwane, 15, 41, 147, 191
Priggee, Milt, 23, 54, 118, 228

R

Ramirez, Mike, 14, 37, 58, 64, 72, 98, 121, 144, 193, 205, 231, 236
Ramsey, Marshall, 7, 14, 47, 105, 130, 161, 170, 237
Reiner, John, vi
Rogers, Rob, 43, 71, 96, 146, 191

S

Sack, Steve, 5, 22, 65, 66, 70, 89, 96, 103, 111, 112, 153, 175, 180, 201, 205, 217, 226
Schorr, Bill, 43, 59, 101, 129, 194, 199
Scott, Nik, 29
Sheneman, Drew, 6, 22, 30, 72, 107, 119, 133, 199, 201, 216
Sherffius, John, 68, 81, 167, 185, 211
Simanca, Osmani, 32, 83, 85, 88, 90, 133, 229
Singer, Andy, 20, 25, 55, 124, 201
Sorenson, Jen, 163, 173
Spencer, John, 28, 49
Stahler, Jeff, 23, 149, 163, 194, 211
Stantis, Scott, 14, 62, 107, 121, 158, 170, 188, 224, 225
Stayskal, Wayne, 48, 60, 130, 174
Stein, Ed, 8, 14, 71, 147, 156, 188, 203
Streeter, Mark, 116, 119, 146, 147, 150, 165, 191, 213, 233, 236, 238, 241
Summers, Dana, 39, 47, 58, 70, 101, 109, 140, 177, 199, 206, 223

T - U

Thompson, Mike, 10, 16, 31, 51, 55, 73, 80, 98, 103, 118, 161, 166, 168, 179
Trever, John, 6, 15, 71, 106, 119, 125, 163, 165
Trinidad, Corky, 109, 146, 155, 187, 217, 223, 233, 235, 237

V - Z

Varvel, Gary, 100, 103, 157, 166

Walters, Kirk, 52, 82, 168, 170, 221, 223, 231
Wasserman, Dan, 39, 151, 160, 188, 210, 227
Wheeler, Shannon, 9
Wilkinson, Signe, 30, 61, 117, 140, 155, 176
Wolverton, Monte, 18, 69, 119
Woolf, Marie, vii, viii, 204
Wright, Dick, 22, 46, 78, 112, 130, 158, 164, 177, 219
Wright, Larry, 4, 30, 46, 53, 55, 177, 194, 209

Zyglis, Adam, 130, 166, 195, 219

ANTONIO NERI LICON, Mexico